BOOMER UNDER

THE BAOBAB

And other published writing of

Charles Dumas

© copyright 2012
BURNING BAOBAB PRESS
State College, PA.

Boomer Under The Baobab
and other published writing of
Charles Dumas
Independent Press
ISBN 978-1-4675-3899-290000

Dedicated to Mom, Dad, Granny, Grandpa, Great Grandma Daisy, Alison, Mr. Crown, Mrs. Barnett, Uncle Willie, and all of the other ancestors whose shoulders I stand on and whose hands have lifted me up.

ISBN 978-1-4675-3899-2
90000>

9 781467 538992

Author's Note

One of the reasons I came to Penn State University back in 1995 was to write a book. I was going to call it: *Nontraditional Casting*. It was going to be about my life as an actor, writer, and director. I had just finished performing in a major action-adventure film, *Diehard With A Vengeance*, which starred my friend Sam Jackson and Bruce Willis. I had also made my Broadway debut going on for Frankie Faison in the revival of *The Shadow Box*. Those accomplishments, along with being in two national commercials, led me to believe that I had something to say that might interest a few people. My agent thought I was nuts.

"You don't leave New York at the height of your career to go teach in the middle of nowhere," she told me. So when do you go teach, I thought, when you are at bottom of your career?

I imagined myself sitting under a tree, presumably a Baobab, surrounded by eager young novices taking notes as I eloquently shared the pearls of wisdom, gathered from a lifetime of experience in show business. I saw myself retiring to my study in the evening to write the book. It was an idyllic vision. I figured my year-long appointment as a guest artist in the theatre department would be just about enough time to complete a couple of drafts of the memoir. Seventeen years later a rough draft of the preliminary outline of *Nontraditional Casting* gathers dust in my desk drawer. Recently I notified my agent. I am retiring from professional theatre. However, I will still be teaching eager young would- be artists though not under a Baobab tree. Baobab trees do not grow in Central Pennsylvania.

A few years after I accepted a tenure- track position at PSU, I became the Arts and Entertainment editor at *Voices of Central Pennsylvania*. I reviewed plays and movies, talked about trends in the art world and occasionally wrote about politics and social issues. *Voices* published some of those articles in a series called *Democratic Conventions, A Bellwether of Our Times.* I have included an excerpt from the series in this book .

No one who writes a book does it alone. I want to thank all of those people who helped me, inspired me, taught and shared their stories. I must begin with my beloved wife, partner, best friend and most courageous supporter, Dr. J. Ann Dumas.

I want to thank my dear friend Herb Newsome. He provided the cover design and other graphics. Like the surrogate son that he is, he came through again in the pinch as he always has.

I am not the first published writer in the family. Daisy Dixon, my paternal great grandmother produced a chapbook of inspirational poetry back before I was born. As always I stand on the shoulders of ancestors.

This book would not exist were it not for my friend and editor, Mary Haight. She helped me gather a bundle of loosely disconnected notes, articles and stream of consciousness utterings into something resembling a cohesive work.

Art Goldschmidt helped me get my job at *Voices of Central Pennsylvania* and Bob Heisse hired me at the *Centre Daily Times*. I thank them for their confidence in me.

In 2009 I started writing a monthly column for our daily newspaper, called *Under The Baobab*. A friend noted that if I wrote enough columns I would ultimately have a book. Many of the articles included here are edited versions of that column. Eureka. I hope you enjoy it.

Charles Dumas, PSU, May 2012

Table of Contents

MISCELANIOUS WRITINGS

HOPE AND PROMISE
Is the beauty in a field of snow
made ugly by a leafless tree?
There are some who say it's so
when they talk of me.
But when the Spring comes
as surely it must do,
What then shall these people say?
The tree alone will blossom true.
The snow will have melted away.

WHAT IS A BAOBAB ? *Centre Daily Times (CDT) March , 2009*

I picked the name *Under the Baobab* for my column because it has a special meaning to my wife and I. In West Africa, elders meet under Baobab trees to discuss the affairs of the village. The elders call the gatherings but everyone who has business with the community is welcome. In many ways the gatherings are like Borough Council or town hall meetings. I hope that this column will help provide a "meeting place" for all members of our community. I welcome any and all responses, criticism, arguments, praise, jokes that you are willing to share.

The Baobab tree grows in Africa. If you have seen pictures of the semi-arid regions of Africa you have seen a Baobab. Strange looking trees, they appear to be upside down with their roots pointing toward heaven. They flower when other trees don't and provide a source of water and nourishment in an otherwise barren environment.

Aside from serving as a site for community gatherings, the plant has many other uses – food for animals, medicine, shelter, and building material. Because of its appearance and life cycle, the Baobab is thought to bring nourishment from the heavens to the earth. When we lived in Mali we became very fond of these trees.

Once while driving late at night, we picked up a young pregnant woman who was in labor. Her husband was with her. They were desperately trying to get to the hospital. At the time the infant mortality in

Mali was the worst in the world. One out of every three infants died before reaching their fifth birthday. We sped down the highway. There were no streetlights or highway markers. You could never tell who or what might wander on to the road. Suddenly, a loud crash shook the car. The sky started to get lighter. It was the middle of the night but it seemed as if the sun was rising. We continued to drive, somewhat mystified. We discovered that lightning had hit a giant Baobab tree further down the road. With the tree supplying the needed illumination, we could go faster. The mother's contractions were getting closer together. We made it safely to the maternity clinic. The family got out and continued on with the sacred business of bringing new life into the world.

We never made it back to that region of Mali. That was over twenty years ago. I often wonder whether that child, now an adult, was raised hearing the story - How toubobs (foreigners) came out of the night in their four wheeled drive chariot and drove their pregnant mother to the hospital guided by the light of a burning Baobab. Persons brought into the world under such circumstances might get the idea that they were special. Such special people don't strap on bombs, walk into crowded places and blow themselves up. They know that their lives, all lives, are precious. A child, an African child, who comes into the world like that might have the audacity to dream, to hope, that they might grow up to be a President or Prime Minister. Those kind of dreams sustain hope. May all of our children come into the world by the light of burning Baobabs.

Mending Nets , *CDT, August, 2009*

I told one of my young relatives that I wrote a column for our newspaper. He said, "Why would anyone want to know what you have to say?" Defensively I responded – "because I am an elder with a lot of experiences and a bit of wisdom." Then I realized that my senior citizen status is the primary reason that most young people dismiss anything I have to say, unless, of course, the information "will be on the final."

Up the Senegal River in West Africa on a fairly large island there is a fishing village. On the windward side of the island, shaded by a circled grove of Baobab trees, the elder men gather when they are no longer able to go out on the fishing boats. They mend the nets, which harvest the fish, which sustain the economy of the village. Without those strong nets the village could not survive. While working they tell stories about their days on the boats. They repeat oft told tales about the ancestors and origins of the families of the village. If a problem arises that the young people cannot handle, they bring it to the grove and ask the advice of the gathered elders. The young are not bound by the advice of the elders but more often than not they heed it.

Children are in the grove, the ones who are not ready to go out on the boats, or to cut mangos or to grow food, or to sew or to cook. They run errands for the elders and bring them water and tea. They listen to the stories and thereby learn about their culture and history. By the time they go out on the boats, they have learned most of what they need to know about who they are.

In our Pennsylvania communities there are many elders. They are not gathered under Baobab trees. They live in retirement facilities and nursing homes. They gather on park benches and on senior Mondays in local diners. You see them at matinee performances, sporting events, lectures and sometimes in continuing education classes. Most of them are retired. We don't ask them for advice, unless they are powerful or rich. Our obsessive pursuit of power and money, particularly during the last thirty years, has helped us to bury ourselves in a dismal economic hole. In the process of "getting and spending" we have truly lost our powers. Maybe we should visit our local Baobab grove to ask our elders if they know how to get out of the hole. They've been there before.

Charles and Coretta Scott King during the 1980 election

FREEDOM

The Fourth of July, *CDT, July 2009*

The Fourth of July is my favorite holiday, the celebration of our country's birth. Of course, the United States hasn't always been OUR country. At the time of its creation, many, including some of my ancestors, were not seen as citizens or even people. So I don't celebrate the beginning. I celebrate the courageous struggle of the countless generations of ordinary people who came after daring to dream of a land where freedom was the rule, not the exception. They helped to grow the American dream from its bitter roots.

I celebrate the original inhabitants of this land who continue to fight to maintain their culture against the onslaught of foreigners.

I celebrate the Africans who struggled for freedom and when given the opportunity, helped to build a better land for their children.

I celebrate those who put their lives on the line to sustain a union free of the tyranny of oppression. And I celebrate those GI's in later generations who went abroad to free others from tyranny.

I celebrate my colleagues who stand for an hour each week to witness that our country is still not free of war.

I celebrate the women who marched and the men who walked with them, so that all could be citizens no matter their gender.

I celebrate the union organizers who committed their time and sometimes gave their lives, to ensure that all workers receive fair wages and the dignity to enjoy them.

I celebrate the immigrants who came to this country seeking an opportunity to make life better for themselves and their family.

I celebrate Woody Guthrie, Pete Seeger, Paul Robeson, Odetta, Oscar Brown, Willie Dixon and the other artists who inspired us to believe that –"this land is your land, this land is our land."

I celebrate the young and the old who work the polls and the streets to ensure that everyone has a vote and that their vote will count and mean something.

I celebrate the social workers, community organizers, teachers, clergy and all of those who commit to building a society where justice is more important than profit and every man, woman and child has access to life, liberty and the pursuit of happiness.

Frederick Douglass, the great American liberationist and resistance leader, once spoke at an African-American church in Bellefonte just before the Civil War. He did not like the Fourth of July. He thought it was hypocritical that a country founded on principles of freedom kept one-fifth of its population in chains. Last month Congress got around to agreeing with Douglass. They apologized for slavery and racial discrimination.

I wish Douglass had been able to witness that apology and some other events of our time such as the election of President Obama, the inclusion of ethnic minorities and women in the Cabinet, in Congress and on the Supreme Court. I think he might have had a change of heart and joined me in saying - Happy Birthday, United States of America.

Juneteenth, A Celebration of Freedom, *CDT June, 2009*

Juneteenth had its origins on June 19, 1865. The Union General Granger landed at Galveston Texas, and announced the end of the Civil War and freedom for the people held as slaves. It was two and a half years after Lincoln's Emancipation Proclamation. It was thirty-one years before a Supreme Court decision, Plessy vs. Ferguson, said racial separation was permissible and eighty-nine years before the Court reversed itself in the Brown vs. Board of Education decision, which brought an end to legal racial discrimination. In matters of freedom time moves slowly, particularly in the South.

Before the Second World War, my father left his home in Vicksburg, Mississippi. He never returned. For years he wouldn't tell me why. Sensing that his reluctance was racially based, I told him that things had changed. There was a black mayor, a black congressman who was good friends with the President. It was no use.

A few years before he died, he told me the story. As a kid during the depression he had witnessed the lynching of his best friend. Lynching was commonplace in those days and sometimes carried out under the color of law. A mob had taken the boy to the Courthouse and hung him. After stripping grisly souvenirs from his body, they left him to rot in the sun for three days. His mother had to beg permission to bury her son. A week later, Dad hopped a freight north to Chicago, never to return.

I visited that same courthouse this past summer. It is now a Confederate Museum. The records have been moved across the street to the new courthouse. As we searched through the dusty files, a clerk, who happened to be a black man, led me to some older records. After a few more hours of searching, I held a marriage license issued in 1877 to the grandparents of my great grandmother. Since both had been born in slavery, this was probably the first document that certified their legal existence as human beings under the laws of the United States. For an earlier legal proof of their existence I would have to search through the property records of their slaveholders, or bills of lading for the merchant vessels, which had captured, labeled and shipped their ancestors as cargo. There are no bibles inscribed with family information. Slaves were not permitted to own anything. It was against the law to teach them to read.

The surnames they used were more than likely the surname of their former owners. That was the practice of the time. There was no harkening back to the forgotten names and practices of an African past. Though they were the first legal residents of our line, they were not the first of their kind in this country. There had been generations of their forbearers who had been brought to America to till the soil, pick the cotton, wet nurse the babies and build the houses and courthouses.

I can imagine them standing before the bar, these great, great ancestors of mine, twelve years out of slavery, holding hands and hearts, ready to embrace America, the land of their birth, and hold it to its promise of freedom. Happy Juneteenth !

MLK in State College *CDT, February, 2009*

"In the last few days my organization has been working in Selma, Alabama., where we have centered the struggle mainly around the right to vote... for almost 16,000 Negroes, and only about 250 are registered to vote, not because they don't want to register, but because the registrars absolutely refuse to register Negroes as voter... If democracy is to be a reality, this problem must be solved." –Rev. Martin Luther King

These words are from the speech that Martin Luther King gave at Penn State on March 21, 1965 to over 8,000 people. Three weeks later, he led the Selma to Montgomery March petitioning for the right to vote. Six months later, President Johnson signed the Voting Rights Act. At the time only 19 per cent of the eligible African-Americans in Alabama were registered to vote in contrast to 70 per cent of the Whites. The rest of the South had similar statistics. A little over twenty years later, in 1988, the numbers had changed dramatically. In Alabama 68 per cent of African-Americans had their franchise restored. Twenty years after that, in 2008, a rainbow coalition of black, white and brown Americans elected Barack Obama, a black man, president of the United States.

Black folks have come a long way in forty odd years. But, that is not the whole story. We as Americans have come a long way. Archaic ideas about racial inferiority and the need for segregation are laughable to our children. Racism is headed to the bin where we store other anachronistic idiosyncrasies, like dial telephones. One wonders what MLK would think of the events of the past few weeks. He would have certainly celebrated the inauguration of our new president, but then what?

He would probably have rolled up his sleeves and gone to work on the problems of our time. Too many of our children: black, brown and white do not have the opportunity to achieve all that they can in our great land. He might say that good and fair housing, health care, and education should be treated as rights not privileges. That a fair, just and equal wage for everyone regardless of gender for work done was long overdue. He would see that we are sending more young men to prison than any other country except China. He couldn't help but notice that many of our poorest families are headed by young poor women who themselves grew up in poor families headed by women. He might seriously question the wisdom of conducting foreign wars to protect domestic tranquility. He might be concerned that we have abandoned so many of our elders to a life of impoverishment and despair. He might notice that we have created a scarred, bruised, and warming earth that requires our immediate attention.

So what might King do? He might suggest we begin by remembering and honoring the journey we have already taken. You can't know where you are going until you take a look at where you have been. Members of the State College Borough Council are proposing that a street be named in honor of Dr. King. Hundreds of cities in the country have a Martin Luther King Street or Boulevard. Most are in Black neighborhoods. We really don't have any Black neighborhoods in State College. So of necessity it would have to be a street in a different kind of place. Though he was a modest man, I think Dr. King would appreciate that.

Proposed by Council member Peter Morris, April 2012 the Borough of State College passed an ordinance that renamed a plaza on Fraser Street after Reverend Dr. King

Charles in Vicksburg, Mississippi
Willie Dixon Way

Memorials to Dr. King, *CDT, January, 2011*

A couple of weeks ago my wife and I visited two memorials to Reverend Dr. Martin Luther King Jr. in Washington D.C. The first was sculptor Lei Yixin's magnificent stone structure, *Out of a Mountain of Despair, A Stone of Hope*. The name comes from a line in his 1963 speech during the March on Washington, which I was blessed to attend. The memorial includes a 30-foot statute of King. It rests on a four-acre site near the FDR Memorial along the banks of the Tidal Basin, between the Jefferson and Lincoln Memorials.

The other memorial to King we visited was the Occupy DC settlement in McPherson Park. Several hundred people have set up their own Grange settlement to focus attention on the vast economic inequality that exists between 99 per cent of the population and the super-privileged 1 per cent. The super-rich control over 40 per cent of our Nation's wealth. Twenty-five years ago they only controlled 33 per cent of the nation's wealth according to Joseph Stiglitz in *Vanity Fair.*

These ninety-nine per centers are part of the growing worldwide movement in support of the Occupy Wall Street protests in NYC and other places. PSU students have one in the HUB. It is a new and creative effort to establish forums to address the growing problems of poverty in our nation. The United States has surpassed Brazil, with the greatest economic inequality of any country in the world.

Why is this movement a memorial to King? Many people know of King's work in the area of civil rights and racial equality. Some know of his work speaking out against the war in Viet Nam. But what most don't realize is that in his last years King dedicated his life, to address issues of poverty and economic disparity. In fact, the day he was killed in Memphis he was supporting a strike by municipal sanitation workers.

King tried to organize a movement to force the Congress to pass an economic bill of rights for the poor. It was to include: a commitment to full employment, a guaranteed annual income, more low income housing, universal health care and greater accessibility to education. It would have provided a framework to move our nation toward equality instead of toward greater inequality. To do this he initiated a Poor People's Campaign. Poor people would occupy the mall in Washington D.C.

In 1967, some of us had convened in Miami to plan for the campaign. Later that November a five-day retreat in South Carolina kicked off the effort. Tragically Dr. King was assassinated five months later, just before the campaign gained momentum. Nevertheless, one month after King's assassination, thousands of poor folks, set up Resurrection City on the Mall in DC to provide a people's lobby for the proposed economic bill of rights. The police closed down the tent city a few months later, citing health code violations. Needless to say the economic bill hasn't passed...yet. No one in Congress talks about it. Maybe it's time to resume the conversation.

CONFIRM SOTOMAYOR NOW, *CDT,May 2009*

Some say Judge Sotomayor should not be confirmed to the U.S. Supreme Court because of her judicial "activism", which is code for "she doesn't agree with our neoconservative agenda". They believe that the Supreme Court should only make decisions based on precedents and a strict interpretation of the Constitution except when it relates to selected Presidential elections and the application of the Bill of Rights for some people.

Had the Court blindly followed precedent we could still be under the 1896 ruling of Plessy v. Ferguson, which had stated, inter alia, that Jim Crow racial segregation was legal and permitted. In its 1954 Brown vs. Board of Education decision, the Court reversed Plessy, finding that state enforced segregation was inherently unequal.

In reality, Brown is not the case that concerns most folks. It is Roe vs. Wade. They are concerned that Judge Sotomayor, a Catholic and graduate of Cardinal Spellman High School, if given a chance, might vote to uphold a woman's right to choose. A reasonable assumption given the fact she is being nominated by a pro-choice

President. To paraphrase Senator McCain, during a recent confirmation hearing – there are consequences to winning or loosing an election

The year of the Brown decision, 1954, was also the year that Judge Sotomayor was born. Her working class parents had immigrated to the South Bronx from Puerto Rico. Twenty-five years later in 1979 she graduated from Yale Law School. Thirty years after that our first African-American President is nominating her to the highest court in the land. There are consequences to Supreme Court decisions.

I knew Sonia back at Yale Law School. We graduated in the same class. We didn't hang out. She was Law Review and I was pursuing international law. She was one of the smartest ones in the room; I wasn't.

Some say that Sotomayor should be appointed to the Court because it needs another woman. Women are 50 % of the population but only 30% of the Court. I agree we need more women in positions of power. But I don't believe that is the reason she should be appointed to the Court.

Some say, appoint her because she is Hispanic. She would be the first Latina on the Court. Hispanics will soon be the largest ethnic group in the country. That's true but that is not why she should be on the court.

Some say appoint her because the Court needs a voice that understands and can speak up for the poor and working class. It does but that's not the reason.

I believe Judge Sotomayor should be appointed to the court because she is simply the most qualified and experienced jurist to be considered for the Court during our time. She has served on the federal bench for over seventeen years. She was first nominated by George H. W. Bush, a Republican, and later elevated to the US Court of Appeals by Bill Clinton, a Democrat. She has been an assistant district attorney, a corporate attorney and a vigorous champion of the law and the rights of all people.

She IS the smartest one in the room.

Charles Rangel, *CDT, December, 2010*

Congressman Charles Rangel, is a good man. Last week he stood in front of the House of Representatives as his colleagues voted 333- 79 to publicly censure him. Censure has been used only 22 times in American history usually for crimes such as bribery and support of the Confederacy. The last time Congress took such a drastic action against a sitting member was 1983. A couple of congressmen were censured for having sexual relations with House pages. Rangel was accused of failure to pay back taxes on a vacation villa and soliciting donations for a center being built in his honor.

When the tragic ritual concluded, Rangel simply said, "I know in my heart that I am not going to be judged by this Congress but I am going to be judged by my life. "

Charlie Rangel has done much good for the people of Harlem, and for the disadvantaged and distressed people of our country. During the difficult days of the 1980's, Rangel often stood alone at the mouth of the cave facing the dragon. He gallantly fought to save the gains from the civil rights movement that were under attack, among them: the Voting Rights Act, Legal Services, NEA, EEOC, and others.

I worked for Charles Rangel as an intern caseworker in his Washington office in 1975. He had been a former high school dropout who was reaching out to give another high school dropout a leg up in life's sweepstakes. It was his first year as a junior rep on the powerful Ways and Means Committee. Later he became Chairman. Part of my job was to find relief for constituents in need. For Rangel who served for a time as the head of the Congressional Black Caucus, the Country's entire African-American community was his constituency. He was always accessible to the people. He never hesitated to speak truth to power. A life is not represented by what is inscribed on a stone or scribbled on an edict. A person's life is more like a container whose identity depends on all its contents. Charles Rangel's life may contain some unpleasant sediment but it also runneth over with commitment to public service and goodness.

Charles and Congressman Charles Rangel, Washington D.C. 1976

WE ARE

We Are Penn State, *CDT, Op-ed, November 2011*

I have been a professor at Penn State University since 1995. The same year Graham Spanier became president. I hadn't known him before, although we both grew up in different neighborhoods on Chicago's Southside. We share a common affection for the new nation of South Africa. He was born there. I teach there. He has been a strong supporter of our theatre department in particular and arts in general. He is a good man. He is bright and compassionate. My wife and I consider him and his wife to be friends as well as colleagues.

During Graham's tenure a lot of positive changes have come to Penn State. His commitment, dedicated work and accessibility to students are exemplary. He has been considered one of the finest college presidents in America. It was rumored that he was twice on the short list for a cabinet post.

I don't know the details, but I believe he made a grievous error of judgment in failing to act sooner and more decisively concerning the reported circumstances surrounding the child abuse at our university. Many think his removal by the board of trustees is in the best interest of the University. I don't know. Such decisions are made way above my pay grade. But, I don't think that he is part of a grand conspiracy that consciously allowed a child molester to abuse and torture children. I think it is more likely that a devious sexual predator used treachery and carefully constructed old-boy connections to create opportunities to molest vulnerable children.

Graham is an honorable man, a good father and teacher. He takes those responsibilities seriously. He was also the CEO of a multimillion-dollar institution, the fifty-first most important university in the world, the area's largest employer. He took that job seriously as well. Sometimes those responsibilities do not mesh well. Sometimes you delegate when you should regulate. It was a grievous fault and grievously Graham has paid for it.

I don't know Joe Paterno personally. I have met him a few times. But, I know other members of the family. Sue, his wife, is a Eucharistic minister at our campus service. She was a strong supporter of our State College Shakespeare Festival. My wife and I lived in and paid rent for five years in the first house purchased for the Catholic Student Center, the Suzanne Pohland Paterno Center, helping to subsidize the development of the project.

I don't have to argue for Joe's integrity, works or reputation. His life and good works speak volumes. He is a man of unimpeachable character and a great teacher. His long-term reputation as a coach, teacher, and human being, though tarnished by these recent events will ultimately shine in tomorrow's sunlight. However, as he has admitted, if he had it to do over, he would exercise better judgment and better care in looking after the wellbeing of those young victims. He also delegated when he should have taken action.

As important as they are to the culture of our university, Joe Paterno is not Penn State - neither is Graham Spanier. Our university is - 95,000 students, 45,000 faculty, staff and administrators and almost 500,000 alumni. WE are Penn State. Each of us has a story that contributes and shall continue to contribute to the greatness and also the fallibility of our University. We remain a work in progress. We have a glorious past but that past is not meant to subsume our present. We are currently traveling through a dark valley of despair. With God's grace, it is up to us who love this university, to clear a path to a brighter future. Those who do not know us or care about us, or who hate us should not be permitted to spread their sensationalized manure about us. What should we do?

First, as University Park Undergraduate Association President, T.J. Bard suggested on CNN, our first visible collective action should be to support those children who were victimized on our campus, in our home, at our university. They have been badly injured by a predator. Our hearts, prayers and support must go out to them.

Second, as acting President, Rodney Erickson, said in his letter to the PSU community:

"We are a university that is committed to its core values of honesty, integrity, and community. We are a university that will rebuild the trust and confidence that so many people have had in us for so many years. Through your conduct every day, you can play a role in restoring the pride, integrity and honor that have always characterized Penn State. I share your anger and sadness in this time, but this is the only responsible course to take in the coming months."

Third, we must support the young men on the football team this coming Saturday and in the coming weeks. They did not bring this situation on themselves. They have had to endure under the most difficult circumstances. They still strive for the excellence exemplifying the best that is Penn State. I hope they win. However, winning or losing is not the primary issue. Playing with dignity and behaving with integrity is. That is the Penn State way. It is as important to those fans off the field as it is to the team on it.

Fourth and perhaps most important, this is a difficult time for all of us. It may be the most difficult many of us have faced. We are all hurting. Let's make sure we take care of each other. We shouldn't rush to vent our anger, or give in to despair or fix blame, especially when we don't know all of the facts. It means going on with our lives and duties even if it seems like "what's the use". It means we should look out for others who might need our help. It means maintaining our Penn State pride and our belief that the good that we do can live on after.

Joe Paterno died two months after this was published. As of this writing Graham Spanier is suing the University to get access to his emails for a potential defense in a civil action. Sandusky was convicted of multiple counts of child molestation. The football team played its heart out but lost the last two games. Before the first game after Joe Paterno was fired, players from both teams took to the center of the field to pray for the children who had been abused. It was a candle in the darkness.

Chaos or Community, *CDT, January 2010*

This column marks the first anniversary of *Under The Baobab*. I am honored that some of you take time to read my meanderings and that some have given feedback and appreciation. Thank you.

The column was inspired by a need to share my thoughts about our world. As an elder, I have become accustomed to becoming invisible in our youth oriented culture. The past and our observations about it are often treated as irrelevant, unless that past is being sampled as part of a new hip-hop pop hit. In this column, I have tried to express an elder viewpoint that is rarely heard or printed. It is not just my perspective. Truth be told, I get my ideas for columns from you - my neighbors, my friends, my community.

A community is a group of people interacting and sharing a common environment and common interests. We all live in a global environment where unilateral actions create reactions that can ripple to the cosmos. A carelessly thrown match can ignite a forest fire, which can create smoke containing carbon dioxide, which collects in the ozone layer, and contributes to global warming. A fanatic tried unsuccessfully to light a shoe bomb on an airplane. As a result millions of people must take their shoes off before boarding a plane.

Now another misguided young man has tried unsuccessfully to sabotage a plane. Most likely, the result will be a factor in the transformation of airline security measures and a further increase in airport tensions. Millions of hours will be lost. Passengers will be forced to endure intrusions into their personal space and violations of their privacy. More chaos. We will put up with it because we value security. But is it more important than liberty? In a viable community, liberty and security should co-exist in balance.

To build that type of world community, we must first recognize that we are living in the same "neighborhood" We have common interests and common responsibilities. It was the young man's Muslim father who advised the authorities that his son was a potential hostile belligerent. He put the interests of the community before those of his family.

Next we should sit down, talk, and work out our differences. We will need tolerance and understanding. We are all living on this earth and we have to learn to share it.

Finally, speaking of the global community, this week would have been Martin Luther King's 81st birthday. It has been forty-five years since he spoke at Rec Hall at Penn State. My dear bro', Dan Walden was there. Isn't it time that we commemorated that historic event by naming a street after him? Almost every city, town and hamlet of comparable size and importance has a Martin Luther King street or boulevard. Why not State College?

Now Fraser Square will be renamed Martin Luther King Square

The Village, *CDT April 2009*

Eight years ago, April 23, 2001, a group of Penn State students "occupied" the HUB/Robeson Building to call attention to issues of race. They called themselves –The Village. It was not the first time that students took over buildings at the University. In 1969 Penn State students occupied the telecommunications building to protest the Viet Nam war and racial discrimination at the university. Veterans of that time report that the University administration reacted as if they were under siege by hostile forces.

In 1964, I was part of a civil rights group in Oakland, California that was recruiting students at UC-Berkeley to protest the racist hiring policies of the local daily paper. The paper's publisher, a UC-Berkeley trustee, demanded that the university shut down our recruitment table on the campus. It resulted in a series of confrontations that led to the Free Speech Movement.

Four years later I was part of a theatre activist group that protested Columbia University's attempts to annex parts of the Harlem Community. The University sits on a hill above the community. They wanted to build a gym at the bottom of the hill. Members of the community protested the move as oppressive gentrification. Some of the African-American students occupied Hamilton Hall in solidarity. Hundreds of white students occupied several other buildings in sympathetic protest. Columbia called in the New York City police. Hundreds of students were arrested. Some were beaten. Prosecution replaced pedagogy in the name of restoring order. In the 1960's and 70's other student protests were followed by even more disastrous results. The National Guard opened fire on a protest at Kent State killing several students. Student protestors were killed at Jackson State, Mississippi and in Orangeburg, South Carolina.

At Penn State in 2001, the administration and the protesting students in the Village did a strange and wonderful thing. For nine days they sat down together and talked about the problems and their mutual concerns. During that time students attended classes, took exams, wrote papers. At the end of the day they returned to the HUB/Robeson Center to sleep over. President Spanier and Vice Provost Jones, negotiating for the administration went about their duties each day preparing for graduation.

The students and administration reached an agreement. The Africana Research Center was established. There was an increase in faculty positions in the African and African-American Studies Department. Additional courses and scholarships were established. By sitting down and talking with each other these potential adversaries, created an environment of civility and diversity at Penn State.

Later that spring my wife and I went to a centenary celebration of her great grandfather's graduation from West Point. During a question and answer session the Academy's commandant was asked whether the cadets were required to take any courses in ethical behavior. He responded, " Yes, we talk to them about ethical conduct. But, we don't sit down and have discussions. This is West Point not Penn State." I have never been prouder of our university.

Four months later on September 11th the world was turned upside down by the attacks on the World Trade Center, the Pentagon and in Pennsylvania. Since then we have stopped talking to each other. War, torture and terror replaced negotiation. Maybe it's time we followed the example of the children of the Village and started talking again.

Not Here, Not Now, *CDT, July 2009*

Most Americans celebrated the election of President Obama. It was an indication of how far we have progressed in race relations. From a society erected on the enslavement of one race of people by another we have evolved into a country where a member of that formerly enslaved race could become president. We are on the road to recovery from the debilitating pandemic of race dominance. Last week's incidents remind us that we may be on the road but we haven't reached the destination.

Professor Henry Louis Gates, a prominent African-American scholar at Harvard, was handcuffed and arrested in his home. One of his neighbors in Cambridge called the police when she saw two black men pushing against Gate's front door around noon. When a police sergeant arrived he found Gates inside the house. Gates had just returned from a weeklong project. He explained that he had come in through the back door because the front door was jammed. The policeman demanded identification. Gates produced his driver's license and Harvard ID.

What followed is in dispute. But what did NOT happen was that the policeman did not tip his hat, apologize, and ride off into the afternoon. He apparently expressed some suspicion that Gates could be the owner of this fine Cambridge home. Gates apparently expressed some annoyance at being harassed in his own home. The policemen arrested Gates. A minor scandal you say, but it couldn't happen in State College.

Last spring break, late one Sunday night, I drove to the Carnegie Building to pick up my wife where she was working. The campus was deserted. As I waited for her, someone drove by and stared into our car. I waved and smiled. They moved on. Jo came out, and we drove the three blocks to our home on Atherton just past Park. A police car started following us. As we made the left turn into our driveway, the police turned on the car's flashing lights and siren. Two other police cars appeared, lights blaring, blocking our egress. I started to exit the car; I was warned to get back in and remain still. Jo being less used to such police tactics than I, attempted to get out on her side. She was warned to stay in the car. The police searched through the car with their flashlights. I handed over my license and PSU ID.

When I asked, "what was wrong, officers?"

I was told curtly that I had made a right - hand turn into the left lane. We were the only cars on the street at that hour. They asked whether this was my house. I was tempted to say it belonged to the bank but curbed my wit. It was painful. It was humiliating to be treated like a criminal, in your home, in front of your wife. But, you learn, as a Black man in America, to just shut up if you want to survive. They verified my ID and drove off. Not here? Not now? Not Yet.

Save Webster's, Save Ourselves, *CDT July 2010*

This was going to be a column about why I had chosen a black actor to play Stanley in State College Community Theatre's forthcoming "A Streetcar Named Desire" at the Boal Barn. But something more important came up. (Still, go see the play in late July. It is going to be very interesting). On Tuesday I got an emergency e-mail from Peter Morris, a member of the State College Borough Council. Webster's Bookstore Café on Allen Street was in danger of being evicted by the end of the month. An impromptu meeting was being called. A few hours later, almost 90 people showed up to support Elaine Meder-Wilgus, the proprietor.

If you don't know Webster's, you probably don't live in State College. If you haven't been there in the past few months, you probably should leave the house more often. For some of us Webster's is part of the sinew and muscle of this community.

At the meeting, someone said, "this is the only place in town where everybody feels comfortable meeting anybody." A fellow faculty member said it was the only place where he could talk with his undergraduate students comfortably. Another person said it was the only place that her teenage daughter would be seen with her.

The make-up of the attendees was a testament to the diversity of the bookstore's clientele. All kinds of folks hang at Webster's, all races, ages, gender types, classes. It is the only place in town where a professor might have a conversation with a homeless person or Democrats regularly debate Republicans. It is where anti-war protesters agree with ROTC candidates about their mutual support of the troops. Someone suggested we all write letters about what "Webster's means to me."

Truth be told, I am one of the regulars. When I go downtown, I stop at Webster's to get a cup of coffee, meet friends, find an obscure book, hear a play reading, listen to poetry, enjoy live music, see local artists' work, munch on a homemade muffin, purchase fair trade coffee, have a meeting.

I first came in contact with Webster's when Elaine let us hold our Monday play readings at the store. Later I had a book signing and a couple of poetry readings. Many times I went in just to surf through all the books I haven't read while sipping coffee. Recently, when Toni Morrison came to Penn State, Webster's was the only place in town that had hard-cover copies of all of her novels - at a reasonable price.

Aside from writing letters of appreciation, we didn't know how to prevent the eviction. Elaine emphasized that the landlords weren't bad people. We shouldn't cast them as the villains in this play. In our postmodern world, we tend not to be divided between heroes and villains. Rather we are divided between those who act and those who sit by and watch. If we sit and watch Webster's disappear, our community will be diminished for it.

We didn't sit by and watch. Some people got very active. In April 2012 Webster's reopened in larger, better facilities on Beaver Avenue. It is even busier. We experience a lot of set-backs these days but this time the community won one.

Open Community, Open Hearts, *CDT, October 2009*

The first time Jennifer came to State College's Centre House, a program of Housing Transitions, Inc. (HTI), she was 13 years old. Her parents were separating. She and her mother were homeless. Centre

House provided them shelter as they did for 111 people last year. The second time Jennifer came to Centre House, she was pregnant. HTI provided her with shelter, and also economic and social support as they did for 2,364 other people last year. They helped her to enroll in classes at Penn State. The third time she called on HTI for help, her daughter, Auja, had been born. HTI helped her get a permanent residence in the community. After Jennifer graduated from PSU, she secured a professional staff position at the university.

Jennifer's story is an American success story with a happy ending. Her success came because of her tenacity and courage and with the support of Housing Transitions Inc. HTI nurtured three generations of Jennifer's family. It is only one story. There were at least 2,364 others last year in Centre County.

Many of us are unaware that our neighbors have problems finding a place to stay or feeding their families. We mistakenly believe that poverty does not exist in State College. If it does, it is someone else's problem- the government's, the churches', anybody but ours. At the core of some of the major issues of our time: health care for all, education of our children, a sustainable environment, drug and alcohol addiction, crime control, and war, is a self-centered materialism. A myopic vision that limits our perception of our neighbor's condition and our collective ability to solve these problems. Global and local issues require inclusive and comprehensive solutions. We cannot ignore the poor, the marginalized, and the disenfranchised and expect to prosper.

My wife and I lived in a small village in Mali for a while doing research. At the time Mali was one of the five poorest countries in the world. Yet in that village no one was homeless or hungry. Everyone, no matter how young or old, belonged to a family, and through the family was connected to the community. Yet in the U.S., the most prosperous country in the world, we have people who have become disconnected from the community.

What can we do? First, support organizations like Housing Transitions Inc. It is announcing a planned expansion of Centre House on November 5th. Be there to learn more about it. Send a donation. Volunteer some time.

Second, we have a local election coming up for Mayor, borough council and school board members. Vote for candidates who do not just promise a better life for the already well-to-do and lower taxes for the wealthy, but vote for candidates who have demonstrated that they care about the people, all the people, in our community. Finally, open your heart and listen to the muffled cries of the poor in spirit, body, mind and means. Your caring may be the support they need to write another great American success story.

Give Peace a Chance, *CDT December 2011*

As the U.S. withdraws the last combat troops from Iraq, activists from the State College peace group are ending their vigil. They have been a presence at Allen and College since soon after the invasion of Iraq in March 2003, standing in witness for peace each Wednesday afternoon.

"The war is over. It is time to refocus our energies and efforts," said one of the activists.

Another one said, "Of course, it is a bitter-sweet victory. There is still a war in Afghanistan."

Usually from six to twenty people attend the vigil. Many have been coming since the Iraq war began. This Wednesday they will gather for the last time.

Originally called Operation Iraqi Freedom, the Iraq War began when the United States, under President Bush and Great Britain, under Prime Minister Tony Blair, along with a few smaller countries formed a coalition of forces to invade Iraq. The stated purpose was to remove Saddam Hussein, then president of Iraq. Another major goal was to eliminate a potential threat to regional and world security. Secretary of State Colin Powell asserted before the UN Security Council that Iraq possessed or was developing weapons of mass destruction (WMD). Despite an extensive search, none were ever located in Iraq.

Some US officials also alleged that Hussein had harbored and supported al-Qaeda, the terrorist group identified as responsible for the attacks on the World Trade Center and the Pentagon. Evidence of that connection was never established.

The Iraq War was one of the longest in US history and one of the most expensive. The government spent over a trillion dollars. Billions of dollars were paid pursuant to no bid contracts with Halliburton (where Vice-President Cheney had formerly been the CEO). Tens of billions of those dollars were lost, stolen, unaccounted for, or otherwise missing.

The human toll was even more tragic. Almost five thousand US troops were killed. Over thirty thousand were wounded. This does not include those with psychological injuries. Thirty per cent of US troops who were deployed experienced serious mental health problems within months of returning home. Over ten thousand Iraqi police and soldiers have been killed. ABC News reported that over one hundred thousand Iraqi civilians have been killed. Four and a half million Iraqis have been displaced inside Iraq or forced to emigrate to Syria or Jordan.

One goal was met. Saddam Hussein was deposed, arrested and ultimately executed by the provisional Iraqi government. It was a costly assassination. Is the threat to regional security eliminated? The country has held several elections but the government is still unstable. According to a poll, 82 per cent of Iraqis are strongly opposed to the presence of coalition troops. 67 per cent feel less secure because of the occupation and less than 1 per cent believe that coalition forces are responsible for any improvement in security.

Someone wiser than I once said, in war there are can be no winners. The peace activists on the Wednesday vigil bore witness to that truth.

SPIRIT OF CAHIR SHOULD LIVE ON, *CDT August 2009*

Fall used to be my favorite season. It promised new beginnings. It is the season that students come back to school, bright eyed, full of energy, expectations and hormones. The theater season also begins anew each fall. We anxiously look for the new August Wilson, Wendy Wasserstein or Charlie Smalls.

Lately for me, autumnal memories have made the season bittersweet. It was in the fall, more than 10 years ago, that I watched my father, who had given most of his life in service to his country, drown in fluid spewing into his lungs from cancer. It was in the fall, five years ago, that the heart of Alison, our oldest daughter, filled with love and compassion, exploded in her chest after a routine operation. During other autumns we lost friends like August Wilson, Wendy Wasserstein, Charlie Smalls.

This last week, though it is not quite fall, we mourned the death of Bill Cahir. His untimely death under enemy fire in Afghanistan left our community bereft of a true patriot. He was killed attempting to secure a safe environment for that country's national election.

Bill was a 1986 graduate of State College High and 1990 honors grad from Penn State. At Penn State, he was a columnist for The Daily Collegian. I first met Bill and his wife, Rene, when he was running for Congress last year in the Democratic primary. He didn't win, finishing a respectful second in a three-person race. Those who should know say that had he chose to run again, he would have won easily. But, instead he chose to serve his country in a different way. A Marine sergeant, he signed up for his third tour of duty.

He went there so that other people in other places might have a chance to experience democracy, so that other children would have a chance to hope. Sometimes those of us who have issues with war in general and that war in particular, fail to recognize the sacrifices of our young heroes who answer their country's call to duty. It is easy to forget that while we oppose the war, we should honor the warrior. Last Sunday, several hundred members of this community came to celebrate and to honor a very special life. We sipped lemonade and told stories. We embraced and tried to comfort Rene, pregnant with two children who will never have a chance to know their father in the flesh. We as a community should make sure that their father's spirit remains alive.

If you would have a better world, teach your children well, the poets tell us. Those of us who teach, must teach the young that it is honorable to serve their country. As I prepare for yet another Fall beginning I hear the chorus of Dad, Alison, August, Ted Kennedy and, most of all, Bill chanting the truth of their experience. They echo the words of Arthur Miller from an earlier era, they say -- teach and nurture the children, but remember -- they are all our children.

Mayor Welch, CDT, *September 2009*

I came to State College in 1995. Bill Welch is the only mayor of the borough I have ever known. It is a testament to his integrity as a political leader that I was here for five years before I knew his party affiliation. In truth, he wasn't a Democrat or a Republican or even an Independent. He was the Mayor. Both parties nominated him in the upcoming election. Members of both parties sought him out for advice.

During those years I also didn't know if he worked for Penn State or in the private sector - he WAS the bridge between gown and town. He respected the dignity of all- townies, students, and visitors. I knew him not just as mayor, town ambassador, and public servant. Our families shared meals in each other's homes. He was one of my first mentors and advisors in the local political scene. He always advised me to act in the spirit of service not partisanship.

He presided over the Borough Council with the same grace and dignity with which he conducted his life. This community and our family will miss him terribly. He was an irreplaceable pearl of no price. Now we must try to get along without him. He has taught us well through his leadership and example.

Rest in peace, my friend, knowing that the world you lived in was one that you, more than most, helped shape.

Coquese Washington, *CDT March 2010*

At Penn State, we are blessed to have some of the finest coaches in America. This year some of them stood out. The whole country knows about the legendary Joe Paterno, whose football team just won him a record twenty-fourth-bowl victory. In fact, the Maxwell Football Club just announced that they will be creating a special Joseph V. Paterno award.* Everyone knows about Russ Rose. His women's volleyball team won their third straight national championship, an unprecedented feat. Ed DeChellis' B-ball boys won the NIT Championship last year. Coach Erica Walsh's women's soccer team has won twelve straight Big Ten Championships. But I believe the most impressive job was done by a coach whose team didn't win a championship or even finish near the top in national rankings - Coquese Washington, head coach of the women's basketball team.

She came into a program that was on the brink of disaster. A national scandal had rocked the rafters. Unhappy players had transferred and filed lawsuits. Disgruntled fans had abandoned the team. Students recruited by one person to play under one system found themselves playing under another. The national media looked for ugly stories in ugly places. The team had several tumultuous years trying to make the transition from that crisis. Under less sturdy leadership, the women's basketball program could easily have fallen apart. The students would have suffered. But Coach Washington guided the ship and stayed the course with patience, compassion and hope. She shaped those young people into a team. Coach Washington led the Lady Lions out of their cocoon into the competitive world of Big Ten basketball. They had their first winning season in a while. In Indianapolis, they won their first Big Ten Tournament game. In the second round they led at the half before succumbing to a hot shooting Iowa team (that ultimately lost the final to Champion Ohio State at the buzzer). The Lady Lions like their coach never quit.

In college sports, winning and losing isn't everything. It is not even the most important thing. It is teaching young people how to face adversity, how to show up ready to compete and to give your all. That builds character. It teaches them to play well with others, creating teamwork. When you teach them to play hard and play fair they learn integrity. Helping them to continue to struggle even when the odds are against you tempers courage.

Most of our young scholar athletes will never play professional sports, but they will go on to contribute to our society as citizens, professionals, workers, business people, and teachers. The coach's primary task is to prepare our young people for those future roles in life. They provide it through leadership and example like Coach Washington.

This past season the Lady Lions returned to the sweet sixteen and won the regular season Big Ten Championship

*Because of the Sandusky scandal and Penn State's response, JoePa was fired. The Maxwell Football Club rescinded the decision to create a Paterno Award

JoePa *February 2012*

Like many Americans I first heard of Joe Paterno when he turned down a lucrative financial offer to coach professional football in order to remain a teacher at Penn State.

I next encountered him when I came to Penn State as a guest lecturer in 1995 and decided to stay. I grew to love teaching. When I met Coach, I was surprised to note how this giant of a man was relatively small in physical stature. I was also struck by his humility and accessibility.

I met other members of the family. I got to know his partner, the love of his life, his wife, Sue. She came to mass and distributed communion at the university's Catholic services. She even came after football games, whether Penn State had won or lost. She was one of the generous supporters of our Shakespeare at The Palmer Theatre Company giving donations but more important her time. Jay, his son and assistant coach asked me to speak at a Democratic Party rally during which the Grateful Dead performed.

The Paterno Family are ardent supporters of our community. The Paterno Library extension and the Suzanne Pohland Paterno Catholic Student Faith Center bear their name but a hundred other projects that they helped to build and support do not.

To me JoePa made his greatest contribution as a teacher. My wife and I were fortunate enough over the years to have about thirty football players in our classes, including two starting quarterbacks. The players were usually near the top of the class in academic performance. A few went on to have careers in professional football but all went on to get their degrees and mature as young men and citizens.

Paterno had a plan and his players stuck to it. He told them they were good citizens first, students second, and football players, third. You didn't mess with the Paterno plan. If you failed your courses or misbehaved in the community or violated school or NCAA rules he would bench you, whether you were a star player or not.

One of my favorite Paterno stories revolves around Wally Richardson, who was Penn State's first Black starting quarterback. He was having a rough season. In one game, Joe benched him and brought in another player, who miraculously brought the team back from defeat to victory. The next day the press and fans were all over it, talking about - the quarterback controversy at Penn State.

Joe shut them up with, "No, controversy, Wally is my starting quarterback.". A coach bent on just winning would have made a different decision, potentially crushing that young man's spirit. But, Joe was a teacher, first. He knew that benching Richardson under those circumstances could easily have damaged his self confidence for life.

That was JoePa, after God and his family, his students came first. We the community and the world will miss him. We will never see his like again. We are all blessed to have shared this all too brief time with him.

This was the last article I submitted for my column in the CDT. Sadly they didn't publish it because I had announced my intention to run for

Congress and the editorial staff decided it might be a conflict of interest. I did put it on my blog. Another Paterno story has to do with Adam Taliaferro, a young player who was injured during a game. He was paralyzed from the neck down and his prognosis for recovery was dismal. Joe made sure that Adam got full support and whatever medical attention was required. He kept the young man's situation before the team and before the public. I was privileged to do the voiceover for a promotional video, BELIEVE, when the football season was dedicated to him. Adam finished school, graduated law school. He is now one of the alumni representatives on Penn State's Board of Trustees.

A Time for Every Purpose Under Heaven, *CDT January 2012*

This is a time for healing. We are hurting, brothers and sisters. We are passing through a dark and devastating period. For many it is the worse they have experienced in their young lives. Rev. Martin Luther King's birthday falls on January 15th, so this month I usually write about his life and work. King understood people who are hurting. He tried to heal the wounds caused by racial discrimination, war and economic inequality. It is appropriate to consider how he might approach our present situation. In our polarized political atmosphere, would he counsel even more confrontation? Would he suggest even more consumption-based programs to solve the growing national economic inequality? In cases of the child abuse would he suggest retributive revenge?

King was assassinated while fighting for the economic rights of low-wage sanitation workers in Memphis. In this struggle, he applied the Gandhi inspired tactic of Satyagraha, soul force, or nonviolent resistance. King said, "Darkness cannot drive out darkness; only light can do that. Hate cannot drive out hate; only love can do that." He understood we must not simply transfer power but we must transform hearts.

In our present situation, he might suggest we avoid assigning blame for past ills but seek creative solutions to our present problems. He might suggest the way out of our habits of overconsumption is to consume less, and find ways to recycle our unused stuff. There are no quick and easy solutions to the hurt suffered by young people in our community, the victims of child abuse. For our students, sound bites will not repair the shattered reality of their beloved university.

South Africans handle some of these problems differently. Although we are an older developed democracy and multicultural society, we can learn from them. Because of their recent history they do forgiveness and reconciliation a little better than we do. A few years ago some privileged white students at a prestigious South African university publicly humiliated a group of black domestic workers in order to protest the school's integration policies. They videotaped the incident and put it on YouTube. It caused a worldwide scandal. People saw the incident as a return to apartheid. They demanded the students be punished. Ultimately, the rector (president) of the university was forced to resign.

Last year, the new rector Professor Jonathan Jansen, one of the more enlightened and creative educators in South Africa, tried something different. He brought the students and the workers together, instituting a reconciliation process in an effort to heal everyone's scars. He invited the offending students and workers to sit together and talk. They ate together and prayed together. In the end the students apologized and the workers accepted their apologies. The process was documented in a dance narrative called *RACE, RECONCILIATION AND THE REITZ 4.* Several of the artists who produced the piece have been invited to recreate it using Penn State student dancers. It is to be presented at the Playhouse Theatre on Sunday, January 22nd at 7 pm. Maybe they can show us how to begin to heal. It is time.

Thinking Rock at The University of The Free State

THE LARGER COMMUNITY

The Reitz Four, *CDT, March, 2011*

Three young white men, neatly dressed in suits and ties, entered the packed auditorium. Former students at South Africa's prestigious University of the Free State, they had come for their public punishment. Back in 2008, they had perpetrated the notorious Reitz Four incident. Humiliating four black domestic workers, they videotaped the event. It was put on YouTube creating a worldwide scandal coming from a country whose recent past had been mired in apartheid. But these boys were not repressed bigots manifesting their desire to return to a racist past. They were born and raised after apartheid ended in South Africa.

The domestic workers, dressed in their Sunday best, entered the hall. The dignitaries present, included the university's rector (president), a former chief justice of the National Supreme Court, members of the Human Rights Commission, and the local mayor. Scholars and faculty from various disciplines, had spent the day in a seminar discussing issues such as discrimination, separation, alienation and reconciliation. South Africans take racist behavior very seriously.

This event began with a personal message from Nelson Mandela. The Bloemfontein Children's Choir sang, "We are the children of Africa. We are building the rainbow nation." Another choir sang the Lord's Prayer. There were speeches, lots of speeches. Then came the main event. The former rector came to the podium and apologized to the workers on behalf of the university for allowing such an atrocity to take place. Then he apologized to the boys and their parents for the school's failure to teach them the fundamentals of what it means to be a true citizen of a multicultural society.

One of the boys, speaking for all, directly addressed the workers. He said the workers had always cared for them with affection and trust. He said they had betrayed their trust with their shameful act. He begged the workers' forgiveness. Everyone anxiously waited as two of the workers came to the podium. Speaking in their native tongue and addressing the attackers as "our children who we must embrace and teach," they said the magical words: "We forgive you."

Cameras flashed, the crowd applauded. The choirs burst into song. An elderly woman dressed in traditional garb, a Christian sangoma, gave her blessings and passed candles to the workers and boys alike "You are showing us what can happen in the light of forgiveness." The workers and boys tearfully embraced. This ceremony of reconciliation reminded us they are all our children, rich and poor, black and white, including these miscreants. We have a responsibility to build them a decent world and show them an example of how best to live in it.

Just down the road from Penn State sits Rockview prison, which also "houses" young people. Most of them were no older than our students when they entered prison. Unfortunately, they have a different curriculum. But, let us remember -they are also our children.

Oprah in Africa *CDT, July 10, 2011*

When she walked into Callie Human Hall at the University of the Free State (UFS) in South Africa, the audience of over 5,000 people erupted as if a rock star had just appeared. Moments before, 200 of us had formally marched in wearing academic regalia. We were there to honor Oprah Winfrey as UFS presented her with an honorary doctorate. It was the first she had received outside the United States. Oprah smiled and waved happily to the crowd.

After the formal presentation, she spoke informally to the audience. Some had anticipated surprise gifts, as was typical of her talk show. Her talk was the most cherished of all possible gifts. She told us of growing up in rural Mississippi with a dream of doing something special with her life. As one of the most influential people in the world, she has people as diverse as President Obama, Nelson Mandela, Beyonce, Bill Gates, and Toni Morrison on speed dial.

She spoke about talking with then-President Mandela about opening a school in South Africa. Madiba immediately called the minister of education. She donated $40 million and organized the staff and faculty. At the investiture she was hailed as a daughter of the soil of Africa. That is really only partially correct. I believe she is daughter, mother and sister to the entire world.

She told us how special it was to receive an honorary degree at this particular university, which had excluded black people during the apartheid era. She called the university's transformation into one that is open and inclusive of all students a modern miracle. She praised Jonathan Jansen, the rector, as a special leader and educator. She talked about how the Reitz Four students, who had made a racist YouTube video in 2008 that embarrassed black domestic workers, had been transformed through a process of truth, forgiveness and reconciliation. She brought the workers on stage and called them heroes.

She spoke for over an hour. The audience was transfixed with her wisdom, her transparency and her love. She answered a few questions from the audience.

One student asked respectfully, "Why was the Oprah show the most popular talk show for 25 years?"

She replied, "You are looking at the reason — me. I took care that every show would be something special, which helped people."

Afterward students told me that this event had changed their lives: "She's a billionaire, the most powerful woman in the world and she chose to visit and talk to us."

"I am at your university because I chose to be here. This is a very special place" she told them.

Ateqnohkew Pemohneau, *CDT, June, 2010*

A couple of years ago Stan, an elder of the Menominee People in Wisconsin asked his friend Richie Plass, a member of the tribe, if he knew the origin of his Menominee name, Powekonnay.

"Yes," Richie replied, "it means one who changes his feathers."

"Did you know that it was the name of the chief that led our people during their removal from our ancestral home to their present location on the reservation? Though 2,400 started out, tragically only 1,600 arrived safely. "

Richie hadn't heard that story. After researching it, he decided to recreate the trek of 76 miles that the Menominee were forced to walk during the winter of 1852. Another elder named the Walk – *Ateqnohkew Pemohneau –a walk that tells a sacred story.* Richie gave it a purpose: "to educate others about the hidden history of our people and to fulfill a sacred responsibility to the ancestor whose name I bear."

On June 2nd, ninety Menominee, members of other Native American peoples and their friends gathered at Lake Poygan. Richie was "gifted" a pipe by some of the spiritual leaders. It was considered a sacred trust and high honor. The elders conducted a ritual to honor the creator and ancestral spirits. Sacred stories were revealed. The next day a dozen or so people set out on the Walk. It would take five days, covering about 18 miles a day. The walkers followed the Wolf River as closely as possible, the route of the original group. They camped out at night. At times the Walk was difficult. Several of the walkers were over sixty years old.

But, as Charlotte Kinepoway said, "We need to walk in their shoes to experience what our ancestors did. We need to honor them. Without them we would not be here."

There were several signs that the ancestors were truly with the Walk. Each morning, after the group prayed, large flocks of geese flew over heading north, the direction the group was marching. After the group arrived at the reservation, a large golden eagle, a symbol of the Menominee, landed high in the trees and observed the ceremony. It was considered a good sign.

Others had joined the Walk along the way. Ateqnohkew Pemohneau transformed some lives. One young man, a veteran from the Iraq war, suffering from PTSD and in trouble with the law, took it upon himself to carry the sacred staff and to lead the group for two days. At the end, everyone agreed, he was a changed man.

The Walk ended at Wayka Falls with prayers, celebration and feasting. Young singers praised the 50 or so people gathered there. Richie tearfully thanked each of the walkers as they ate a traditional meal of wild rice, deer meat, corn, squash soup, bread, and smoked sturgeon, a fish sacred to the people. Because of dams and other intrusive technology, sturgeon have all but disappeared from the Wolf River. Thanks in part to Richie Plass the Menominee have not. Perhaps, now as the Menominee retell their old stories and celebrate their ancestral beginnings the sturgeon like the Golden Eagle will return.

Shalom, *CDT, September 2010*

Shalom, Prime Minister Netanyahu.

Salaam, President Abbas.

Mr. Abbas, we have never met.

Mr. Netanyahu, we met once, years ago in the Fox News sky box at the Democratic National Convention in Atlanta. You were not yet prime minister. You were in Atlanta as a guest of Rupert Murdock, head of News Corporation. I was there as a technical assistant working on electrical connections for what was to become Fox's first full telecast of a national political convention. You were talking with Murdock, Barry Diller and a couple of other folks who lived way above my pay grade.

You did a curious thing. You came over and talked with me. You were very gracious. You asked about my job, my family, where I was from. I looked into your eyes and saw a good man. You initiated a conversation. That rarely occurs between people from our diverse circumstances. We talked for a few minutes. Then Murdock called you back over and I went back to my work. I have never forgotten that meeting and having a chance to talk with a celebrity who treated me, a technical assistant, as a fellow human being.

For many years I have actively protested my own country's involvement in wars in the Middle East. I have kept my opinions about the situation between Israelis and the Palestinians to myself. I would not attempt to dictate to a sovereign people how to conduct their affairs. A nation should determine its own destiny as it forges a relationship with its neighbors. However, in our complex world, where we share the common space of the shrinking earth, we have all become neighbors.

This is not a diatribe about Israel's right to exist. Israel has an indisputable right to exist. Anyone who believes otherwise is a fool Fools should not be allowed to set the political agenda. But, it is also indisputable that the Palestinian people should live in a country where they have political representation and a voice. Both your peoples, indeed, the world's people will never find lasting peace until both these realities become real.

It took courage and vision for the two of you to come together and sit down in the same room. I urge you to gather courage to take the next step. Look into each others eyes and realize your common humanity. If you can do that the rest -land, settlements, Jerusalem, immigration, right of return can be worked out.

We Jews, Christians, and Muslims, are the spiritual descendants of Abraham. It is time for us to come together and say as did those true heroes of the last generation – "from this day forward to forever there will be no war." We must strive in our hearts and with our hands to make peace. Shalom.

The Social Evolution in Egypt, *CDT February, 2011.*

Last week as we shoveled our way out of the mid-winter snows and braced ourselves against the near record cold, the people of the second most populous country in Africa took to the streets and transformed their future. Thousands of Egyptians marched and demonstrated. Despite what seemed to be a period of prosperity, they demanded that President Mubarak step down. He finally did, causing a great concern for the Obama administration.

Over forty years ago another American president, Johnson, was concerned about Egypt's political situation. Thousands of Egyptians had taken to the streets shouting the name of their president, Gamal Nasser. Israel had just soundly beaten the larger and better equipped Egyptian Army (along with the Syrian, Jordanian and Lebanese armies) in six days. Nassar had resigned in disgrace. Yet the people were in the streets screaming their support for him, even though he had led them into a total and abject defeat they still wanted their leader. It is a window into the Egyptian national psyche. Nasser rescinded his resignation.

Because of its size, strategic location and relationship to the Soviet Union, Egypt created major problems for the Johnson administration. Several years passed before another Egyptian leader, President Anwar Sadat, and Israeli Prime Minister, Menachem Begin, in the presence of President Carter shook hands and vowed to never again allow their two countries to face each other in armed conflict. We celebrated that moment at Camp David. We have supported both countries over the years with billions of dollars in aid.

Now another American president sits by as the situation in the Middle East deteriorates. Hampered by wars and rumors of other wars, he lacks the resources to intervene even if he wanted to. It's to bad the Nobel Prize didn't come with an instruction manual on how to negotiate peace.

We should return to the side of the angels in the middle-east. Mubarek is gone. He could not survive the peoples' cries for freedom. We can only hope, that in his wake, a new peace will emerge. We must allow the will of the people to manifest, not just in Egypt, but in Afghanistan, Iraq, and Palestine. It is time for us to stop using our military might to police the world as the British did before World War II. It was a bad idea when they did it then; it is an even worse idea for us to do it now. Economically and spiritually, we cannot afford to create new wars or to continue old ones. It is time we tried peace.

Project Haiti, *CDT, February 2010*

One of my favorite nieces, Ceci is going to Haiti. She teaches school in New York City and has volunteered to spend two months this summer helping the children of that ravaged country.

I am proud of her.

I am afraid for her.

Haiti is the poorest country in the Western Hemisphere. 80 per cent of the population lives below the international poverty level and 54 per cent live in abject poverty. Less than half of the population over fifteen can read and write. Those were the country's vital statistics before the recent earthquake which killed 200,000 people and left a million homeless, out of a population of 10 million.

I first visited Haiti back in the 1980's at the behest of Archbishop John Cardinal O'Connor of New York. I was conducting research on the life of Pierre Toussaint who was being considered for sainthood. I was writing a play about his life. It was during the regime of the dictator, Baby Doc Duvalier. He was very rich; most Haitians weren't. They were poor, very poor. Haitians worked in sweat shop textile factories for less than a dollar a day making clothes for US retail outlets. Hard working, they ran to their jobs at sunrise, dreaming of a time when things would get a little bit better. The most resourceful cram themselves into rickety boats. They launch themselves on the treacherous currents, hoping to make the beach in Florida. They still believed, that they could make the world better for their children..

The next time I went to Haiti was with Penn State's Project Haiti in 1997. My wife and I accompanied Project Haiti's founder, Father Fred Byrne, and several dozen students during spring break.

We took three trips to Pondiassou, a remote village in the mountains. We worked on various projects: agricultural, educational, arts and crafts and prayer, lots of prayer. The Brothers and Sisters of The Incarnation, a Haitian Catholic order committed to uplifting the poor through prayer and hard work, ran the projects. In recent years, Project Haiti has focused on an orphanage in near-by Hinche. As of this writing we don't know the condition of our brothers and sisters in Pondiassou or that of the children in Hinche.

Despite my concerns, Ceci will go. Her father was born in Haiti. She has other family members there. She will help rebuild, reconstruct and reconnect. She will try to use her skills and ingenuity to uncap the rich wellspring of Haitian faith and hope. They will help resurrect their country. Ceci and her generation are inheriting a world filled with tragedy and travesty wrought by man and nature alike. Fortunately, they seem to understand that they must mold it into a place that better serves its people, all its people. They deserve our prayers and support.

Ceci's photo project which she developed with the children of Haiti has become a model for interactive community development.

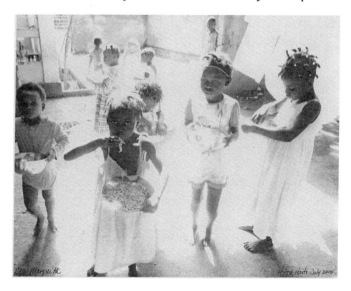

From Ceci's project work in Haiti

Ken and the family at the PSU Lion

LIFE, DEATH, TAXES

A Man's Glorious Life, *CDT, May 2009*

It wasn't a surprise. Ken had been on life support for three weeks and had been seriously ill for months. When his wife, Mary, decided to end his misery, her sister, my wife was there. So were his four children, his two siblings, family and friends. Everyone was there … except Ken. He had departed long before.

I had seen him a week earlier. He was ready to go then. But he couldn't abandon his family. Their youngest daughter was not yet in high school and the oldest, had a year left in college. They were a loving family, lots of hugs and laughter. They hadn't yet figured out how not to be a family. A week before Ken passed, the family rabbit had died, creating a hole in the family. It was difficult but they dealt with it. A man is not a rabbit. A man has things in his life to which attention must be paid. A man like Kenny doesn't leave behind a hole. His passing creates a canyon that cannot be filled, not even by the rivers of tears flooding from the hearts of all who loved him.

He had wooed, won and wed Mary. He provided for her and their family, not just financially or socially. Ken provided the kind of supportive environment that helped his children feel secure enough to risk blossoming in a sometimes hostile world. What Ken didn't understand was that he had already done all that is humanly possible to create that kind of a home. His children will be nurtured to a compassionate maturity. He may have discovered that truth during those last weeks as they came to see him, talk to him, pray with him.

But, as I said, Kenny wasn't really there. His last days, hours were not for us, not even for himself. He was waiting until his family could find the strength to let him go. That was his last heroic gesture. He kept life in those shuddering pounds of diseased flesh long enough to let his children and his wife get ready to say goodbye. Only then did he let go and let God.

On the anniversary of his death we attended a memorial lacrosse game at Whitman High, Kenny's alma mater. His youngest starts school there next fall. Next week his daughter graduates from college. His widow, Mary, is taking classes to become a professional caregiver so she can provide comfort to other grieving families. What do you say when a man dies? You say, thank God he lived and he lived gloriously.

Mary, Ken's wife, graduated from the University of Maryland this past May. She earned her MSW and is working as a social worker in a senior home. His oldest daughter graduated from college and is working as a writer. His oldest son has graduated and is working in health care. The other kids are progressing well. The family is struggling but thriving.

Good Health Care is a Right, *CDT, April, 2010*

For us the spring was heralded not by singing birds or blossoming crocus but by the sighs and sobs of mourning loved ones Herb's death was unanticipated but not unexpected. He had lived 72 years and fathered 26 children, who gave him 32 grandchildren who have had 21 great grandchildren so far. Most were around him at the wake along with a host of friends. It was a great ethnic wake filled with stories, greeting the long-lost, family pictures of just - met cousins, tears and laughter, lots of laughter. Herb had lived fully. His death, though tragic, was the culmination of a full life.

There was no laughter among the people gathered around the brain dead body of Corey Donahue. He was 33 and leaving behind a widow and a twelve-year old son. Two weeks earlier he started getting severe headaches. He should have seen a doctor. But Corey, an unemployed seasonal construction worker, had no health insurance. Seeing a doctor would have meant an economic hardship the family couldn't handle. A week later the pain became so severe that his wife, Tammy, insisted that he go to the emergency room. They sat waiting, while the staff treated the cut and bruised patients before him. Tammy believes they were not seen quickly because they were poor and uninsured. After several hours Corey decided the wait was useless. He went home.

A couple of days later, he started to convulse. As his son, Corey

Junior, tried to help him to the car, he collapsed. He had a brain aneurysm. At the hospital, as the doctors prepared to operate, he was given tests. They showed a flat brain scan. Nothing more could be done for Corey. The decision was made to harvest his organs. It required a forty-eight hour wait before the "life" support apparatus could be disconnected. Doctors said that if Corey had been seen when he first started getting the severe headaches, most likely, his life could have been saved

During the wake we told stories about this vibrant young man. His mother, Gigi, had opted for a home birth with a midwife largely because she had no health insurance. Midwives are cheaper than doctors. We drove her to the emergency room because of complications. They might have been avoided if she had adequate prenatal care. But, she had no health insurance. I remember holding the infant Corey soon after his birth, a miracle baby. Gigi was not at Corey's bedside deathwatch. She died a few years ago. She needed a liver transplant.

The Affordable Health Care Act finally passed by the Congress and signed by President Obama is not just a bunch of words and numbers. It is not a political football to be tossed about in the fall elections. It is about people and families. It was too late for Corey and Gigi and their family, but thank God not for the rest of our children.

As we are editing this book, the Supreme Court of the United States has decided in a 5-4 decision that the core of the Affordable Health Care is permitted under the U.S. Constitution.

Death and Taxes in Postmodern America, *CDT August 2011*

She lived within a five mile radius on Chicago's Southside all her life. But, her spirit reached the four corners of the world. She was an unwed teenage mother who dropped out of high school. But, she raised her son so that he was able to graduate from the same school as four presidents of the United States. She was an only child who bore an only child yet she was mother to a neighborhood and leader to a community. She never held public office above that of election judge but she helped to organize a campaign to elect Chicago's first black mayor. It laid the ground work for the campaign of the country's first Black president. She was never rich, yet her heart and her resources were always available to those in need. She was what Jesus called the salt of the earth and she never lost her savor.

Sitting in the funeral parlor making arrangements for Mom's funeral, I noticed a sign on the director's desk. It read, _the State of Illinois will no longer contribute any funds for the burial or cremation of public aid recipients._

"How do poor people bury their dead?" I asked

"They don't," he replied. "Unless they have insurance, the bodies stay in the morgue for a while then are thrown in a common grave with no marker, no ceremony, no recognition. "

We finished the arrangements for Mom. It included a private viewing before the ceremony so that we, the family, could say good-bye. It is a courtesy not afforded the families of the poor. The morgue does not allow viewing or visitations.

This is what we have come to in postmodern, post recession, post human America. Some of our fellow citizens can't afford to bury their dead. Funds are not available for these "luxuries". Others like teacher salaries, arts education, and child health care are greatly reduced or eliminated. Funeral services for the poor used to be financed through taxes. But, no politician would dare advocate the need to raise taxes, particularly the taxes of their rich campaign contributors. It is easier to cut services, like burials for the poor.

In the last budget debates, the Republican party that controls the House of Representatives and includes our local representatives proposed a plan - no new taxes for the rich, cut spending. They told us the economy would rebound? Yes and pigs can fly. The United States lost credibility on the world's debt market and the stock market took a nosedive. Liechtenstein is now considered a better credit risk than the United States.

Let's get real. It's time to raise taxes so we can pay off the debt, and restore needed services like Medicaid, Medicare, education and funeral services for the poor, for God's sake. To paraphrase the words of a man who knew what he was talking about: this is not a Republican issue or a Democratic issue. It is an American issue. Mom knew that.

Everyone Deserves Health Coverage, *CDT, August 2009*

Last year, leaving my office in Philly, I had what I thought were heart palpitations and shortness of breath. I sat down for a minute. When the symptoms did not go away I went to the campus police station. I told the officers on duty that I was feeling a little woozy. Within minutes, two ambulances appeared. I was whisked off to the emergency room where I was prodded, poked and medicated. There appeared to be no immediate crisis, but the attending physician didn't want to take any chances. So, after checking my insurance ID card, I was admitted and shipped upstairs to a room. I had a restless night, being awakened every couple hours for tests. I signed myself out over the hospital's objections the next morning. When I reported the incident to my family doctor in State College, she suggested that I probably had a bad case of gas.

The total bill for my 16-hour hospital stay was more than $22,000 dollars. We wound up coming out of pocket for a minute portion, but somebody had to pay most of that $22,000. The real issue is what happens to those 46 million people who don't have insurance ID cards and whose heart palpitations turn out to be more than gastric. Many people believe that the debate over universal health care is about money or choice. I think it is about public policy.

Back in the 19th century, some of our political and social leaders thought it might be a good idea if all young people got a basic education. They argued that a democracy would work better if its citizens were educated. So public schools were set up and laws were passed making it mandatory for children to go to school. They didn't eliminate other educational programs. You could still send your kids to private or parochial school. You could even educate them yourself at home, if you demonstrated competence in providing suitable training. The government wasn't as interested in how it was done as long as all children received a basic education.

In the middle of the last century, Americans became more affluent in the post-war economic boom. They also became more mobile. They bought cars. The government as a matter of public policy subsidized private automobile travel by building the federal interstate highway system. The government did not provide a car for everyone but it made using one easier. Most families purchased a car, but many, especially the poor, didn't.

Is health care like education or like a car? If it is like education it should be a matter of policy to ensure that everyone has access to adequate care? But, if it is like a car, access should depend on what a person can afford? It seems to be me that the choice is obvious.

Taking Action Against Cancer, *CDT, Oct. 16, 2011*

I have prostate cancer. Or more accurately, I had it until my prostate was removed a couple of weeks ago and, hopefully, the cancer went with it.

I am not alone. One in six American men will be diagnosed with cancer of the prostate during his lifetime. One in 36 of those diagnosed will die of the disease. After skin cancer, it is the most prevalent cancer for men. Although it is not as life threatening as some others, it is still second after lung cancer among cancers causing death among men in the United States.

As a black man in America, my chance of contracting the disease was 67 per cent greater than that of my white counterparts. In fact, of all groups in the world, black men in America have the greatest probability of being diagnosed with and dying of prostate cancer. Ironically, West African men, with whom African-American men have an ancestral genetic link, have one of the lowest incidences of the disease.

My cancer was diagnosed in December after a prostate specific antigen (PSA) test indicated some potential problems. A biopsy revealed the presence of cancerous cells. I was told that there were several possible treatment options: hormonal therapy, external and internal radiation treatments, chemotherapy and a radical prostatectomy. Another option was something called "watchful waiting," which meant taking no action. Prostate cancer among most men in their 60's isn't very aggressive. Some are able to live relatively normal lives with the disease. Also, surgery isn't recommended for men past 65. I had a contract to teach in South Africa. My wife and I decided to wait.

Living with cancer, any cancer, is difficult. Those six months in South Africa were among the most worrisome in my life. When I returned to the States, the cancer had grown worse and my PSA was up. The prostate is normally about the size of a walnut. Mine had expanded to the size of a baseball. The doctor strongly suggested a prostatectomy. We agreed. Fortunately, there was no indication that the cancer had metastasized (spread beyond the gland). We are waiting to see whether there are other issues to be addressed.

The PSA test and the doctor who persuaded me get it may have saved my life. My enlarged prostate was not detected during my annual rectal exam. Aside from occasional bouts with frequent urination, I had no other symptoms. This disease is a silent killer. Often people don't know they have it until it is too late.

In some ways, it is similar to breast cancer. Fortunately, there has been great work to raise consciousness regarding breast cancer. A yearly mammogram has become routine for the well-being of women. Unfortunately, the same attention is not paid to prostate cancer, its detection or its treatment. In fact some medical people have actually recommended that men don't get PSA tests. In the early days such similar advice was given to women about breast cancer exams.

If you are sitting under the baobab and not already doing it, please get an annual PSA test, especially if you are over 40, particularly if you are black. Living with cancer may be difficult but it beats the alternative.

As of this writing I am still clear of cancer.

Leadership punts, new day dawns, *CDT, November, 2010*

There is a large elephant sitting in the House, perched on the laps of power. Republicans are dancing in the end zone. They look forward to winning the Senate and The White House two years from now. Democrats are wondering if they can recover after fumbling the ball.

Should the process by which we select our political leaders be characterized as a game, where winners take all and losers skulk to the locker room? If so, who actually won the "mandate"? Most Americans didn't even bother to vote. Of those who did, a little more than half voted Republican.

I identify myself as a progressive independent Democrat and voted accordingly. I am not anti-Republican. Lincoln was a Republican. Had my slave ancestors been allowed to vote they would have voted for him. I really liked and respected my fellow Yale Law alum Gerald Ford (though truth be told, I voted for Carter). My Dad was in the Army, so we all liked Ike. He had appointed Earl Warren, a former Republican governor of California to be the Chief Justice of the Supreme Court. Under him they declared that racial segregation was a violation of an American's right to equal protection.

There was a time when we voted for folks because we believed that they had a vision and a plan which would make life better for us, our country and for future generations. The vision was a political platform, but the success of the plan required careful consideration, statesmanship, compromise. In our pluralistic society it meant sitting at the table with friends and adversaries to figure out what was needed and what could be done. It was based on discourse, not defamation. Times have changed. Today, we have many crucial challenges: two major wars, a monstrous debt, high unemployment, environmental decay, economic stagnation are among them.

Locally, we have the Marcellus Shale exploitation threatening the environment, rising higher education costs, rising poverty. We need to build a social net to provide minimum basic support for our elderly, children, and others with special needs not of their own devising. Somebody needs to fix social security so it survives.

We need public officials with the courage to tell us the truth about our situation. The only way to fix some of these problems and provide the economic support system that every other industrialized nation takes for granted is to raise taxes.

After this past election, Christmas decorations seemed to go up on Columbus Day. The powers that be, Republicans and Democrats, focused their efforts on winning the next election. Enacting a vision and developing laws and programs, which will benefit all of the people seemed secondary. The last Congress spent more time than most passing legislation: stimulus package, Affordable Health Care Act, regulation of big business, etc. It cost many of them their re-election. There are now new quarterbacks with new game plans. Let us hope that a few of them are also courageous political leaders.

I wrote this article two years ago after the midterm elections. I kept waiting for someone to step up to the plate. No one did. After some prayer, consultation with friends, discussion with my wife, I decided it was time that I tried walking the walk since I had been talking he talk. We decided to enter the race for the House of Representatives, 5th District Pennsylvania.

Charles Dumas, April 28, 2012, Beaver Stadium
Dumas runs the race.

Charles Dumas, Robert Dumas, Tipper Gore

THE ARTS

This I Believe *April 2009 NPR, WPSU Radio*

I believe that theatre has the power to transform people's lives. Back in the fifties, I was one of the few African-Americans at a Catholic boys high school on Chicago's Southside. One day the English teacher gave us an assignment to present to the class either a poem or a Shakespearian monologue. I chose the dagger speech from MacBeth. We were reading the play; it seemed like the path of least resistance.

After memorizing it, I practiced by reciting it for my mother's friends when they came over to play bid whist. Shakespeare was about as familiar to them as Sanskrit. But, they enjoyed seeing me "strut and frut" my time on the stage. For years afterwards, at every family gathering, Mom would implore me to "do that Shakespeare thing".

In fact, I would perform "that Shakespeare thing" for anyone who would listen, except, of course, my schoolmates. They were for the most part Irish, Italian, and Eastern European kids from the west side. In racially divided Chicago, we didn't have a whole lot in common. They were being groomed to follow in their father's footsteps in the trade unions, or the professions, or politics (one classmate followed his father to become mayor of the city). The paths of my white classmates led through such colleges as Notre Dame, Loyola or DePaul.

My path was different. The only reason I was there in the first place was that a priest had taken me off the streets. It was go to school or go to jail, eventually. Back in my neighborhood, my best friend had already taken his second bust for stealing cars. Another had quit school to join the army. A third had quit to take care of his tubercular infected mother. A couple of guys from that old gang of mine were dead having run afoul of a bigger and badder gang called the Blackstone Rangers. At least four girls had dropped out of school because they were pregnant.

When the day finally came for presentations, one by one my classmates got up to mumble various versions of poems by Kilmer,

Frost and Sandburg. They were greeted predictably by muffled laughter and occasional cat-calls. I was the last one called to recite.

As I began my well rehearsed monologue, I punctuated it with large (but, I thought very dramatic) gesticulations and hysterical (but, I thought appropriately intense) utterances. The class got quiet, very quiet. I noticed out of the corner of my eye, a few puzzled glances. I was sure they were thinking, "What the hell is this crazy colored kid doing?" I was struck with terror, but I continued...faster.

I had rehearsed a particularly gut wrenching moan. For one of Mom's friends, the technique had actually brought tears. I had no idea what these guys would do. More out of fear than art, I closed my eyes and moaned. From the back of the room, I heard gasps. Then I knew. They were listening. I had them, by God, I had them.

Then there was a miracle (it was a Catholic School after all). Toward the end of the monologue at the point when MacBeth hears a bell his wife has rung offstage, the school bell rang right on cue! Miracle two – nobody moved. They sat still and listened. This in a School where I had witnessed an entire gym get up to leave when a dismissal bell rang inadvertently during a bishop's speech. When I finished, the room burst into applause. It grew into a standing ovation when the audience remembered that the bell had rung.

As everyone left the room, tears began to flow like water pouring from a busted tenement faucet. I cried tears of joy, tears of relief and even tears of regret that it was all over. For those moments in front of that class, time had seemed suspended. I felt connected to each and every person in that room and through them to every person in the universe.

I would go on to perform professionally in over two hundred plays, films and TV shows, and receive awards and accolades, including an Ensemble Emmy for *Separate but Equal*, a best actor award from Hollywood/Beverly Hills NAACP, Pennsylvania Council of the Arts grant and a Fulbright Fellowship. But, it all began that day when my life was transformed. Today I try to teach young theatre artists how to use their craft to transform their own world.

The Gods Must Be Crazy, Comments on Celebrity *CDT Dec 2009*

The Greeks believed that gods lived on Mount Olympus. The gods kept to themselves but often interacted with us mere mortals, for example: gods started the Trojan War and Zeus took the shape of a swan in order to seduce Leda. For some reason our wise ancestors worshipped these whimsical creatures. We "worship" similar creatures today. We call them celebrities.

Celebrities, like Greek gods, are not like us. They are more beautiful. They are stronger. They live much more interesting lives. They interact with each other in film, on TV, and at those expensive private parties and clubs. They don't mix with ordinary people. It would tarnish their image.

The only celebrity we have living in Happy Valley is the best - ever football coach Joe Paterno. The Paternos do interact with the rest of us. Sue Paterno distributes communion regularly at Sunday mass. Jay Paterno is also a football coach, blends into the pews and is an active Democrat. Joe doesn't come to our church He would draw focus. The Paternos in their wisdom and humility understand that perhaps in church our collective focus should be elsewhere.

Celebrity distorts reality. As we Christians celebrate the visitation of Emmanuel, the media is more focused on the intimate and private details of Tiger Wood's family life. At this time, when thirty thousand more of our sons and daughters are in harms way, our national attention is on the gate crashers at a White House party. Congress is seeking a way to provide health care for 50 million of our uninsured citizens and the highest rated TV show is not on C-span but is the *Biggest Loser*.

In 1980 a South African film, told the story of XIXO, a Khoikhoi man who finds a Coke bottle that has fallen into his home from a plane flying above his village. It is the first encounter his people have had with the modern world. The village is amazed by this mysterious and obviously valuable object. They would like to keep the bottle, but, being good people, they decide to return it to its rightful owners, the gods, who surely must have dropped it accidently.

XIXO's odyssey takes him into the city for the first time where he beholds many wild and wondrous events. He also observes things that make absolutely no sense. He returns to his village. When asked about his adventures, he responds with the title of the film, 'The Gods Must Be Crazy."

Perhaps if XIXO were to observe us, today and our obsession with the private lives of celebrities, he might rightfully conclude that it is not the gods who must be crazy but the rest of us.

Martin Sheen, *CDT, May 2011*

It has been a few years since Martin Sheen and I spent an hour or so on the set of *WALL STREET* talking about our kids. He was having problems with his son. My youngest daughter was going through her own changes. They really weren't children anymore. Both were in full gallop in their own life races. They were successful in their chosen fields but not necessarily in their lives. As I got to know him better, I liked Martin even more. Later we were both arrested with Father Berrigan on a Good Friday demonstration during a political action in New York. Fortunately the misdemeanor trespass case was thrown out of court so there was no jail time involved. Martin is a celebrity with intelligence and good political sensibilities. On the set he didn't act like a movie star. Both of us were just fathers with children who had problems and we had no ready solutions.

Parents understand. When your children are in trouble you can't help feeling that it is you that has somehow failed. You think maybe you didn't give them enough attention. Maybe you gave them too much. You try to prepare them for the world. But the world you prepare them for is not the one in which they will live. Because that future world is unknowable. No matter how tough we think the old days were, we never had our children's problems and stresses

As a teacher, I have learned that a child's character is forged as much by the community and their peers as by their parents.

Parents send us their rough cut offspring to be polished and prepared for the changing world. It is blessed work. By teaching them we help shape society's collective future.

It requires commitment but also resources to do the job properly. As parents we sacrifice. The community pays school taxes, parents and nonparents alike. Lately Harrisburg acts as if the education of our children, particularly on the college level is more a burden than a responsibility. In these difficult economic times, some of our political leaders have seen fit to drastically cut the state's support to higher public education.

We spend more to keep some young people in prison than in college classrooms. In the name of providing jobs, those same leaders prefer giving the shale gas profiteers a free ride rather than giving our students a needed lift. This short-sighted, self-serving political policy promises a dismal future. A few new jobs may be created but a generation of our learners may be unprepared to fill them. Even more depressing is the message we are sending to our young about how little they matter on our list of priorities.

Parents love and value their children. As teachers we do the best we can with what we are given. We are public servants committed to teaching young people and preparing them for the complex and changing world they will inherit. As parents and teachers we can not do it alone. We need our political leaders to understand that our children must be the priority in today's changing world.

Athol Fugard. The Unexamined Life is Not Worth Living
CDT *June 2011*

THE BIRD WATCHERS, Athol Fugard's latest play is set on his family estate thirty years ago. He explores a crucial decision that affected his life and the lives of two of his friends. It is a fictional piece, but Fugard said that the conversations he had with Barney Simon and Yvonne Bryceland "are remembered vividly and are...responsible for the writing of the play."

In the first act, Fugard writes about the day he decided not to go to Jo-Berg with Simon, the Artistic Director of the Market Theatre or to Capetown with Bryceland to direct her as Clytemnestra. Instead he remained in his Port Elizabeth home to work with local black artists. The decision set his life on the course he followed to fame and fortune.

The second act is set in the present. The family estate has been long ago abandoned in reality and memory. The Fugard character has become a palsied doddering old man. Visited by the spirits of his long deceased two friends, they reveal to him the pain his decision had caused them. Compassionately, he creates an opportunity, which allows Yvonne to play the role she has always hungered to perform.

In actuality, Fugard did not remain in Port Elizabeth. He became South Africa's leading playwright and an important voice in the anti-apartheid struggle of the last century. Tonight he is being honored with a lifetime achievement Tony Award in recognition of his contributions both to the theatre and to the struggle. Last week sitting in The Fugard Theatre in Capetown at the world premiere of *THE BIRD WATCHERS*, I was struck by the attention he paid to this transitional moment in his life and those of his friends.

Certainly that day was not the only one he regretted in his life. There are stories of disagreements he had with other colleagues and friends during those troubled times, Zakes Mokae, John Kani. Some wanted him to use his fame as a weapon against apartheid. But Fugard kept himself removed from the political struggle directly. He argued that politics would detract from his integrity as an artist. He told stories about people caught up in the struggle, in the system, in each other, in life. Through those stories the world learned of the inhumanity of racism under apartheid and the degradation it perpetuated.

Last week I watched him delicately spin a yarn which revealed to us an unfinished corner of his imperfect soul. We all have such moments of regret in our lives, particularly those who have sat for a while under the baobab. But, few of us have the courage to open old wounds or the skill to share the process.

Sidney Lumet, *CDT, April, 2011*

At the passing of Sidney Lumet, we lost a great artist and a committed activist. His career spanned fifty years and fifty films from *TWELVE ANGRY MEN* in 1957 to *BEFORE THE DEVIL KNOWS YOU ARE DEAD* in 2007. Other classics like *NETWORK, PAWNBROKER, THE VERDICT, SERPICO and FAILSAFE* ranged in between. His projects went from the *THE WIZ* starring Diana Ross and Michael Jackson and Richard Pryor to *A STRANGER AMONG US* about an undercover policeman living in an Hasidic community to *KING: A FILMED RECORD FROM MONTGOMERY TO MEMPHIS.*

Like Spike Lee, Martin Scorsese, and Woody Allen he was a premier New York City director. His gritty films could be beautiful or ugly, but they were always rooted in the experiences of working people. He once told me that New York was one of our country's only real cities because of its ethnic neighborhoods, multicultural population and tough streets.

"LA doesn't have tough streets." he said, "It doesn't have streets. People have to learn to live together in New York. They don't have a choice. There's no place else to go."

I had the opportunity to work for Mr. Lumet once a week as a regular on the TV series, *100 CENTRE STREET*. I played the duty officer in the jail beneath the New York City Courthouse. I remember the first day on set in Queens. Before we began, everyone had to run their lines. If you hadn't memorized them, rumor was you'd be fired on the spot. We had our words. But that was not the only innovation.

Mr. Lumet had cut his teeth during the early days of television when they used a technique which required three cameras filming all at the same time. It required the director to choreograph the cameras to keep them out of each other's way. The advantage was it allowed the entire scene to be shot without stopping. Other directors use just one camera, which requires different set-ups. This fragments the action and demands major editing. One camera technique is tough for actors trying to maintain a sense of truth. On set the film crew was griping about having to learn this "new" technique. Their anger subsided a bit when someone noted that we had already shot thirteen pages just after lunch. That's at least twice as many as we would have done using a one camera technique.

100 CENTRE STREET only lasted a season and a half. In my opinion, it was just too good for network television. The cops acted like cops, the lawyers were lawyers and the crooks didn't always go to jail. You know, it was like real life. Mr. Lumet was one of the three best film directors with whom I have been privileged to work. I asked him at the wrap party, if I would have a job the next year.

"Charles," he said, "if I'm working, you're working"

Mr. Lumet, keep the tape rolling. I've got my lines.

THE WIZ- *CDT February 2009*

This week, the School of Theatre is performing *THE WIZ* directed by Steve Broadnax. This is not a review of the piece which I am sure will be great. Rather it is my recollection of working with its original creator, Charlie Smalls.

Charlie wrote *THE WIZ*. He was the first African-American to win Tony's for lyrics and composition. He studied at the Julliard School as a teenager. He could play piano, bass, drums, and guitar. He toured as a backup musician with some of the top acts until he found his calling, musical composition. Charlie wanted to tell the stories of his people He wanted to show their joys and sorrows, their pain and their strengths. Mostly he wanted to bring happiness into the world.

In the mid-80's I was hired to be a script doctor on his new project, *MIRACLES*. It was a musical about a young city boy, Jobob, who is sent down South to live with his relatives. A script doctor's job is to clean up a finished script. I found myself combing through several stacks of songs, music, and some disjointed ideas. There was no dialogue therefore no script. I spent the next few months putting those ideas into some kind of cogent theatrical form.

Charlie habitually worked late at night. I would get phone calls at 3:00 or 4:00 am to discuss something we had been working on earlier that day. The job was exhausting but exhilarating. It was one of the most creative experiences of my life. At the time Lena Horne had a one woman show on Broadway. Calling Charlie, "one of our young geniuses", she sang the title song from *MIRACLES* during the performance. I had very little musical experience but I believed we were headed for great things. After all, Charlie had won a Tony with his first attempt at a Broadway musical. I was already working on my acceptance speech.

At some point, I noticed that Jobob didn't have a theme song. There was no musical expression of who he was or what his journey was about. I mentioned this to Charlie, several times. He said he would get to it. As the date approached for the backer's audition, no song was forthcoming. Out of desperation, I did the unthinkable. I wrote some lyrics for a Jobob theme song. Being a script doctor who anonymously rewrites the book is one thing. Writing the lyrics for a song for a Tony Award winning composer and lyricist was presumptuous. One night as I was leaving Charlie's apartment I slipped the lyrics onto the piano with a hastily mumbled suggestion that he should look them over. I skipped out before he had a chance to respond. I fully expected an irate phone call that night. None came. In fact, the song was never mentioned.

About a week later we were in the upstairs room in Sardis for the backer's audition. We needed to raise two and half million for the production. Charlie would explain the story to the potential investors. The actors would speak enough of the dialogue to set up the songs. Then they would sing. The story reached Jobob's arrival down South, Charlie said, "This is a boy who is confused and doesn't know how to get unconfused. So me and Charlie Dumas have written a song that tells how he feels." He looked at me and smiled. My wife said I lit up like a full moon over the desert. We raised only about half of the required financing. The project went on a back burner. A little while later, Charlie suffered a cardiac arrest during surgery in Belgium. *THE WIZ* remained his only Broadway hit but it was not the only happiness he brought into the world. Thanks Charlie.

The Last Poets Reunion, *CDT, March, 2009*

Some people think that hip-hop began with rap artists like Grand Master Flash, Tupoc, B.I.G. They are wrong. The syncopated rhythms and rime schemes that we know as hip-hop began with the drum accompanied story telling of West African griots.

Even in this country, commercial hip-hop had earlier roots. In 1968 a group of young activist artists came together to form a group called The Last Poets. They performed at rallies and demonstrations and made at least one album. Like Sweet Honey in The Rock, Bob Dylan, Joan Baez, Odetta and Pete Seeger they articulated the aspirations of a movement, supporting political and personal empowerment with their spoken word art. When students occupied buildings at Columbia University to protest the school's involvement with the Viet Nam War and the incursions into the Harlem Community, the Last Poets were there. After the 1960's and 70's, members of the Last Poets went the way of many activists- prison, drug addiction, and community work. Felipe Luciano became a union organizer. Years later I worked with Abiodun Oyewole on an arts education program.

On Saturday, March 14, 2009, some of the survivors of The Last Poets came together for the special screening of the documentary, *Made In Amerikkka-Reuniting The Last Poets,* to the delight of the packed house at the Schomburg Center for African-American Culture in Harlem. (There were featured performances by guest artists: Autumn Ashanti and Universal U.) Created by French film maker Claude Santiago, the film captured The Last Poets at a special 40th Anniversary show in France that had reunited five of the seven living members of the group for a one-time performance.

The highlight of the evening was the live performance featuring group members Abiodun Oyewole, Umar Bin Hassan, Felipe Luciano and master drummer Don Babatunde. The group was called back for many encores. The Last Poets demonstrated that they haven't lost a step. Felipe even brought hot sauce to some bland glands by reading a sensuous love poem to the sisters. He reminded us that we had better, "Wake up or we are all through."

UNSTOPPABLE *CDT Blog, October 2010*

Denzel Washington was sighted several times last week. He was in town shooting a film, *UNSTOPPABLE*. It's about a couple of guys trying to stop a runaway train, which was tearing through the central Pennsylvania countryside.

Some of us got to perform as extras in the Hollywood movie for the nonunion rate of a hundred dollars a day, a good lunch and all of the cookies, coffee, and fruit we could consume. If you have any experience with making movies, you know it is mostly "hurry up and wait." It gives you a chance to talk to people you wouldn't otherwise encounter.

We were in Tyrone, a town with its own version of a runaway train. Like many Pennsylvania towns, it has lost thousands of jobs. Factories have closed, others have cut back shifts, and many jobs have been relocated to Wisconsin and China. Economists debate whether or not the country is in an actual depression. Be that as it may some of us are suffering through some hard times. Ed, told me he was laid off after working at the same factory for 31 years.

"I don't know," said Ed, looking at the sky, "I just don't know." I asked Ed if he had considered relocating to find work.

"I have lived here all my life, just like my father before me. I wouldn't know where to go. But my boy is thinking about Arizona."

Mary worked on farms all her life.

"I take care of cows. Don't have a veterinarian's license or anything. I helped bring a bunch of calves into the world. It's good hard work but I like it." She hasn't been able to find a job in her line of work for two years.

Dave made a mistake twelve years ago. He was seventeen. A felony on his record makes finding permanent work difficult.

"When the agency sends me out on interviews, I tell them to do the background check first. Might as well cut to the chase, no sense wasting each other's time."

Eartha is a single mom who sent her daughter through college. She managed to nurture her child's dreams while trying to make ends meet.

"She wants to go into hip-hop. I say, let her. She has her degree to fall back on."

Marie patched her life back together after her husband left her for a stripper. One of the few professional actors on set, her eyes sparkled when she told me that she was going to be on the TV show, *The Good Wife.*

"I am going to be one of Mr. Big's dalliances. Wait until my cheating husband sees who I hook up with- on national television."

We never saw Denzel up close. His train was too far away. A bunch of my students got to work on the film including one who was selected as a stand-in for one of the principles. She was hanging out in the main tent for a week.

A couple of hundred of us plan to have a reunion when the movie opens next November. We are going to have a red carpet party at a theatre in Altoona. Maybe by then we'll have a reason to celebrate.

Denzil is making a career of shooting films on locations in places which are recovering from hard times. His DÉJÀ VU was shot in New Orleans not long after Hurricane Katrina. SAFE HOUSE was completed in Capetown, South Africa last year. It creates jobs and excitement. He uses his celebrity to work for the common good. He first came to the public's notice in the stage and film version of A SOLDIER'S PLAY. The play was produced by the Negro Ensemble Company, where I worked at the beginning of my career. Other notable members of NEC were Sam Jackson, Adolph Caesar, Francis Foster

The First Frances Foster Award *CDT, June 2010*

Sometimes we complain about the lack of progress toward developing greater diversity in our community. But every now and then we get a chance to celebrate our progress. Gilbert Bailey is the recipient of the first Frances Foster Award for Excellence in Acting and Promoting Diversity in PSU's School of Theatre. You may have seen him as the scarecrow in *The Wiz* or as Romeo in the school's outdoor production of *Romeo and Juliet* or in *Smokey Joe's Cafe* or in a half dozen other productions. He has maintained a 3.4 GPA. He is a most fitting honoree for this award. Like Frances Foster he has promoted artistic excellence and diversity with grace and style.

Francis Brown Foster (1924 -1997) was a distinguished actress, stage director, and a founding member of the Negro Ensemble Company. She appeared in or directed more than fifty shows for NEC for which she was awarded an Obie and several Audelco awards. She received NEC's Adolph Caesar Award for Outstanding Lifetime Achievement. She trained at the American Theatre Wing Academy and was in the original cast of *A Raisin in the Sun*, and understudied the roles of Ruth and Beneatha. She played the role of Ruth on the national tour. She was the first African American woman to appear in a commercial on national television. She made her New York City stage debut in *The Wisteria Trees* at City Center Theatre in 1955 and appeared in hundreds of other plays, films, and television shows. She was a member of the Actors Equity Council.

While on leave in 1997 from the Broadway production of *Having Our Say,* she agreed to play Mama in the Penn State production of *A Raisin in the Sun.* It was the first play written and directed by an African American to be performed on Penn State's mainstage. The idea of completing the cycle, playing all three women in *Raisin,* intrigued her. It was the only college production she appeared in during her career. It was also her last play before she died.

Frances came to Penn State because it gave her an opportunity to work with students. She served as mentor and inspiration to students and faculty alike. Many students from that production went on to perform on Broadway, in regional theatre, and on television, and in films. One is a tenured professor of acting at Ithaca College.

Frances helped change the climate for us all. When she performed at Penn State, there were only three African-American graduate students, a handful of undergraduates, and one black junior faculty member in the School of Theatre. Today, due in part to her example and influence, there are six African-American graduate acting students and many undergraduate majors of color. The faculty now includes four tenured African-Americans and one Latino. The School regularly produces plays by writers of color and has become one of the centers of hip-hop theatre in academia. Much of this progress in diversity came as a direct result of the inspiration and pioneering efforts of Frances Foster.

Frances Foster

PRESIDENT BARACK OBAMA

My "Homie," President Obama *CDT-April 2009*

Although we both spent formative years on Chicago's Southside I never really met Barack Obama. By the time he set up his tent in 1985, I had left town to organize voters in Mississippi. We traveled in the same circles but twenty years apart. I remember getting a call about this bright young man who was running for the Illinois Legislature.

"This guy is really special. He's going to shake things up down in Springfield," he said. That was enough to get a campaign donation from me and to cause a blip on my Chi-town political radar.

Chicago is a special place. Just consider who lives there: Oprah, Jesse Jackson, Minister Farrakhan, Michael Jordan. The City even has its own special blues style created by Southerners who made the great migration: B.B. King, Willie Dixon, and Muddy Waters. Harold Washington became one of the first African-American mayors of a major American city by building a coalition of progressive Whites, Blacks and Hispanics. The coalition defeated the Democratic Party machine and transformed the urban political landscape.

Rev. King lived there during his first northern campaign. He called it "the most segregated city in America." It is the city of Da' Bears and the InvinciBulls, who won six NBA championships during the 1990's. Chicago lays claim to two of the longest legendary losing streaks in baseball history. The White Sox finally ended their championship drought in 2005, their first since 1918. The Cubs still have not won. It has been a hundred years.

Chicago is Sandburg's "City of the big shoulders...hog butcher to the world." It is Gwen Brook's city full of "nothing but plain black boys." The late great Studs Terkel never left his beloved city and Al Capone was drug away kicking and screaming by the feds. John

Dillinger was gunned down on the City's near north side leaving a movie theatre, after being betrayed by a lady in a red dress.

Although politics are part of the City's soul, Chicago had never had a serious candidate for president until Obama. Lincoln was from downstate Springfield. In the 1950's Adlai Stevenson, a senator from Illinois won the Democratic nomination twice only to be beaten by President Eisenhower. In 2004, Senator Carol Mosley Braun, the first (and still only) African-American woman elected to the US Senate announced her candidacy for the White House. But like Congresswoman Shirley Chisholm's earlier run, her announcement was mostly symbolic. Everyone remembers the Democratic Convention of 1968 with Mayor Daley's comment that his police were there "not to create disorder, but to preserve disorder."

Barack Obama is the first president in recent memory who comes from a major urban environment. I have never met him. We saw each other after the first debate in Philadelphia. I was a supporter of Hillary Clinton. I thought she would be more effective running against the Republicans. I was wrong. On the night of the debate at Drexel University a bunch of us decked out in Hillary buttons and campaign paraphernalia gathered to cheer on our candidate from a local watering hole near the school. Afterwards as I stood on the corner waiting for the Market Street bus, a motorcade pulled up and stopped at a red light. There was Barack Obama looking at me from the back of a large black van. He stared at the sign I was holding – Clinton for President. Slowly I moved the sign behind my back. He shrugged and pointed to my chest where I had a large Hilary button. Slowly I moved my other hand up to cover the button. He must have thought that was funny, He pointed it out to the person sitting next to him. The light changed and the motorcade launched him into history. My bus was late: it had to take a detour.

My Homie, Barack Obama-Part 2-*CDT, May, 2009*

President Obama and I come from the same neighborhood, Hyde Park-Kenwood, on the Southside of Chicago. It is bordered on the east by Lake Michigan, on the north by the downtown area, on the west by the remnants of Cabrini-Green and on the south by the University of Chicago. The Woodlawn area, which used to be the home of the infamous Blackstone Ranger gang, is on the south side of the University. Even further south is South Shore, where Penn State President Graham Spanier grew up. Graham and I lived within walking distance of each other but in Chicago in the 1950's that didn't mean we were neighbors.

Hyde Park is a multiracial, multicultural, upper middle class community with the University of Chicago as its epicenter. Synagogues, mosques, Baptist, Episcopal and Catholic churches share corners on the same blocks. Frank Lloyd Wright built his famous Robie House there. Enrico Fermi first split the atom under the bleachers of the university's football stadium. Oscar Brown Jr. created his New York bound musicals while entertaining the likes of Paul Robeson and Miles Davis. Gwen Brooks wrote poems in the local library and in 1954 became the first African-American to win a Pulitzer Prize.

Although we came from the same neighborhood, President Obama and I come from different worlds. He is from the University's Hyde Park. I'm from the "across the tracks" community that co-exists within it. The citizens of these two communities share the same streets but not the same culture. They are not divided by race, although most people in "across the tracks" world are black and brown.

What separates these two worlds is poverty and class. I don't use class as a synonym for elegance or the watered down definition derived from a strictly income -based stratification. By class, I mean a person's relationship to the means of production. That is what and how you work, not how much you get paid. A Ph.D. working as a junior instructor may make the same amount of money as a senior clerk at a retail store, but they do not belong to the same class nor do they have the same potential for success.

People in these two worlds comingle. My grandmother cleaned houses in Hyde Park. My stepdad delivered mail. Mom lived in the neighborhood for her whole life, working as a cab driver, waitress, life guard, worker and housewife. My first job was packing groceries and delivering them for the local supermarket.

We went to same Catholic Church but not the same clubs. We shopped in the same supermarkets and ate breakfast at Valois. But, there are other restaurants in the neighborhood I never frequented. I couldn't afford them. I used to pass by Johnny Johnson's house, the publisher of *Ebony* and *Jet Magazine,* on the way to school every day. I never considered knocking on the door. I would also pass the houses of folks who were barely surviving and be invited in for cookies.

State College is also a borough populated by two distinct communities. Many of us live in the community centered around Penn State. But, there is a second community. According to a recent report Centre County is second in the state in its per centage of poor people. Unlike Chicago our second community is composed primarily of white people who are less visible but no less poor. Some are elderly. As in the rest of the country, many live in female-headed households. Many are children. Some live in trailer parks, some in shelters but all are struggling to survive. They serve us in restaurants, in fast food stores, in nonunionized chain stores, and gas stations. They clean our streets and our houses. They cut our grass and our hair. They repair our cars and our machines. They are our neighbors but they tend not to be our friends.

President Obama is committed to bringing people together. He has embraced diversity in its most creative and important sense. One of his hardest tasks may be getting folks from these different communities to sit down together to address some of the major problems facing us all. It must be done but Obama cannot do it alone. We are all in this together.

Reflecting on the long, long road to here, *CDT, Jan. 2009*

Like a million other people, I will be in Washington, D.C. on Tuesday for the inauguration of Barack Obama. I know exactly where I will be when he becomes the first African-American to take the Presidential oath of office. I will be halfway down on the right side of the reflecting pool facing the Lincoln Memorial. It is where I sat in the summer of 1963 along with a quarter-million others, listening to Rev. Martin Luther King Jr. give his "I Have a Dream" speech.

Some of the people who were on the podium with King will also be in Washington: John Lewis, Andrew Young, Jesse Jackson, Nick Katzenbach, Harry Belafonte, Sidney Poitier, Lena Horne. Others have passed on: Ralph Abernathy, A. Philip Randolph, James Farmer, Paul Newman, Stokely Carmichael, Odetta, Adam Clayton Powell.

Most of Obama's team of young lions weren't even born in '63. But that didn't prevent them from achieving this miracle of manifesting America's true destiny. In America, more than anywhere else, people have a chance to achieve their aspirations. They help create the world that they will have to live in.

Forgive us old folks if we take a moment to remember and reflect. It hasn't always been easy. "Life has not been a crystal staircase". A few days after the March in 1963, racists set off a bomb that killed four little girls at a Sunday school in Birmingham. It was meant to send a warning.

"Shut up, stop agitating for change, leave things the way they are."

Three months later, John F. Kennedy, the young president who had come to symbolize change with his New Frontier, had his head blown off in Dallas. It seemed as if the movement, if not the world, was collapsing.

"Stop agitating"

After the March, I joined Project COFO and went with 2,500 other young people, black and white, to Mississippi to register people to vote. Soon after we arrived, fellow project workers, Andy Goodman,

Mickey Schwerner and James Chaney, two New York City Jews and a Mississippi black, were killed by racist police one night on a lonely highway.

"Leave things the way they are"

Malcolm X kept teaching until he was gunned down on a stage in Harlem. There was still Dr. King. He kept struggling, kept preaching until he was assassinated three years later. Then two months later President Kennedy's brother, Bobby, was cut down in a California hotel after he had all but clinched the Democratic nomination for president. Further chaos erupted at the Democratic National Convention in Chicago. Richard Nixon, the man who had lost to JFK, won the presidency. Abernathy took over Southern Christian Leadership Conference; Jackson ran for president.

"Shut up, leave things the way they are," we were told.

But we didn't quit. The Civil Rights Act was enacted, followed by the Voting Rights Act. It gave millions of black citizens the franchise. Shirley Chisholm became the first African-American to run for president in 1972. Jackson ran in '84 and '88. They renamed the highway where they were killed for Goodman, Schwerner and Chaney. Jesse Jackson's son became a congressman from Chicago.

And now, America will be swearing in our first African-American president. He will not stand alone at that podium. His road to that podium has been paved by hard work, hope, and the struggles of countless generations. It has been wetted by the sweat of multitudes. The road has been cleared by the sacrifice of thousands. That podium, that altar, has been cleansed by the blood of martyrs. No he will not be alone. So, I will return to the reflecting pool along with a few other old gray heads to celebrate but also to remember.

INAUGURATION/TRANSFORMATION
A witnesses account of the Inauguration
Voices, February 2009

"America, in the face of our common dangers, in this winter of our hardship, let us remember these timeless words; with hope and virtue, let us brave once more the icy currents, and endure what storms may come; let it be said by our children's children that when we were tested, we refused to let this journey end, that we did not turn back nor did we falter; and with eyes fixed on the horizon and God's grace upon us, we carried forth that great gift of freedom and delivered it safely to future generations."

As President Obama spoke these words, we were like the proverbial tree planted by the waters of the Reflecting Pool in front of the Lincoln Memorial, but contrary to the old song we were very much moved. The President was calling upon us to carry forth "the great gift of freedom". But unlike previous administrations that had announced similar sentiments as a call to an evangelical imperialism. This President seemed to be issuing a call for a movement of regeneration. We need to bring change, but that change must begin with ourselves. At least that is what we Obama marchers in D.C. and billions of others around the world hoped.

We arrived in Washington early on Saturday night to avoid the crowds they told us were coming. Jo and I were lucky we had a relative in nearby Bethesda. Already several thousand people were walking around the city. There were photo ops and parties everywhere: in front of the Capitol, the Washington Monument, Lincoln Memorial, and near the White House (still occupied by you-know-who). The spirit was celebratory and friendly. It was clear that there were many who had never before been to their Capital City and they were going to make the most of it.

The celebratory spirit continued into the next day, Sunday, with the Inauguration Concert at the Lincoln Memorial. It was where King made his *I Have A Dream* speech in 63, where in 1939 Eleanor

Roosevelt arranged for Pennsylvanian Marian Anderson to give her concert when the DAR refused her admittance to Constitution Hall because of her color. It was where countless workers, soldiers, protesters, million man marchers, poor people, religious people, students, antiwar and prowar people had come to petition their government for redress of their grievances. On this day a half million had come not to protest but to celebrate a sea change in American history.

The *WE ARE ONE* concert was spectacular. Wonderfully produced by George Stevens Jr. (who I had worked with on the Emmy Award winning, Separate but Equal). It was a combination Woodstock, March on Washington, Mardi Gras, and a PBS special on the history of American leadership. There were poetic and political readings, opera, rock and roll, country, folk and inspirational hymns, Some of my favorite moments included Tom Hanks reading excerpts from Copland's Lincoln Portrait, Garth Brook's and a mixed choir doing Shout, and Bruce Springsteen and Pete Seeger doing all the verses of This Land is Your Land. Somehow that song never seemed truer than at that moment. I think Pete and Rev. Lowery who gave the benediction, may have been the only ones on the stage who had been there in 1963.

Monday was taken up with our pilgrimage to JFK's eternal flame at Arlington, and his brother, Bobby's, simple gravesite, nearby. They were two men who were killed trying to bring their own form of "hope" to our boomer generation. We also visited some family members buried at the national cemetery. Later we visited another shrine to our time, the Viet Nam Memorial. Later that night about a thousand activists gathered at Dupont Circle to have a purification ritual. We lit incense, chanted and sang songs to chase the "evil spirits" out of the White House. A few threw shoes at a large blow-up caricature of soon to be former President Bush.

This was all prelude to Tuesday, the day of the Inauguration. In the morning, we marched a portion of the way to the Mall carrying the Obama-Biden poster which had adorned the front of our house during the campaign. We gathered a little contingent of State College/PSU supporters. At least fifty other people wanted to take a picture of themselves next to the sign or just the sign itself. There was chanting and singing along the way, a pre-inaugural parade.

We went to our selected spot, on the right side of the reflecting pool facing the Lincoln Memorial. It was where I had stuck my feet in the water during King's speech back in 1963. This time it was a little colder. I had to crack the ice first to dip my foot in. We couldn't see the Capitol except on the giant jumbotron. We were in DC but like everyone else in the world we watched it on television.

Then came the moment that some had traveled thousands of miles and stood in the subfreezing cold to be part of – The Inauguration. Parents held their children up to see the screen. Fathers told smiling babies that they were watching history. Black and white folks beamed with pride. Old people held hands sharing sacred memories. It got strangely quiet. After he took the oath everyone in the crowd that I could see was doing several things in various combinations: laughing, crying, shouting, screaming and hugging somebody. In fact everybody seemed to be hugging everybody. There were no strangers here; we were all part of a community – the American community. Without a doubt this was the most diverse group of citizens that I have ever seen gathered anywhere for a single event. It was also the largest. There were 2 million people in the crowd. Police reported that there was not a single arrest.

"This is the meaning of our liberty and our creed, why men and women and children of every race and every faith can join in celebration across this magnificent mall."

As the President spoke it was clear that he meant to continue America's march toward destiny. "This is the journey we continue today." He sought to transform a political campaign into a social movement, a difficult process. Those of us old community organizers understand that movements come FROM the people not TO the people. Leaders may inspire us and articulate the need and parameters of change, but it is the people who create the circumstances and manifest the mechanisms for transformation through their commitment, struggle and sacrifice.

Washington rode the boat across the Delaware, but it was those shopkeepers and farmers who fired the muskets which brought about independence. Frederick Douglass articulated the horrors of slavery but it was the thousands of slaves who resisted, escaped on the underground railroad, and ultimately picked up weapons to bring their own freedom. Lincoln orated brilliantly at Gettysburg but it was those who fought and died at Gettysburg and Vicksburg and Shiloh who gave those words meaning. King's leadership in the Montgomery boycott inspired us but it was those unnamed and uncelebrated blacks in Montgomery who walked to work for over a year that brought about the end of segregated buses. His words at the 1963 March helped change the world but without the quarter of million people there to witness, they would have been like coins thrown into an empty wishing well.

President Obama, also a former community organizer, understands that change must come from the people not from the leadership. But, he also understands that without a leadership willing to listen and change with the people, the process is doomed.

"...those of us who manage the public's knowledge will be held to account, to spend wisely, reform bad habits and do our business in the light of day, because only then can we restore the vital trust between a people and their government."

We, like the tree planted by the water, listened. We believed that our hope for a better world, though not assured, was once again possible. We had a President who was promising to work for it and two million committed citizens who had come to witness and ready to

"....carry forth that great gift of freedom and deliver it safely to future generations."

From: **THE DEMOCRATIC CONVENTIONS**
Voices of Central Pennsylvania, February 2000 –Part 4
1980 New York City

As the 1980 election approached, it was clear that Carter was in trouble. People thought he was a good man but a bad president. The economy was in a mess and the new Islamic fundamentalist government of Iran attacked the U.S. Embassy and took the staff hostage. Coming so soon after the "defeat" in Vietnam, American machismo was at an all time low. Carter was not a sword rattler but there were those in his administration who were. A bungled military attempt to rescue the Embassy hostages made matters worse.

Meanwhile on the Republican side, another former governor was making a run for the nomination. Ronald Reagan had been an actor and, interestingly enough, a liberal Democrat in his early days. But he ran successfully for governor of California as a born-again Republican who made his conservative predecessor, Senator Goldwater, seem like FDR. To balance the ticket he chose a Yale educated Texan who had been U.N. Ambassador and head of the C.I.A., George Bush.

The Hudson Valley, where we lived, was politically conservative. It had an agriculture based economy until IBM moved most of its domestic operations there in the 1950s. Fewer than 5 per cent of the population was African-American or Hispanic except during the picking season, when hundreds of migrants came North to harvest apples, grapes and other crops. The public schools in Poughkeepsie were being investigated by the U.S. Justice Department for allegedly maintaining segregation in the schools.

The last Democrat to win a major election in the Hudson Valley east of the Hudson River was Franklin Delano Roosevelt in 1912 when he ran for the New York State Senate. He had a great name (his cousin, Theodore, had been President) and lots of money. Although he was a Democrat, he was perceived by the conservatives as "safe." He wasn't. Later most people in The Hudson Valley got so mad at his progressive politics that they never voted for him again. In his race for governor and his four successful campaigns for the Presidency, Roosevelt never carried his home district. Faced with that information, after consulting with my wife, I decided to run for the NYS Senate as a Democrat.

We ran a progressive campaign. We tied it to a get- out- the-vote effort, which even some Republicans applauded. We called our campaign the Rainbow Campaign because we were bringing together all kinds of folks who felt left out of the mainstream. We employed tactics we had learned in the movement: grassroots organizing, emphasizing local issues and demonstrating how national policy affected local realities. We won the Democratic Party nomination. Endorsements came in from the AFL-CIO, other labor, NOW, churches and community groups. All but one of the local papers endorsed us.

With the help of Fritzi Goodman, a dear friend and major party operative, we were able to bolster our campaign by mixing in some high-profile appearances. James Earl Jones headlined a benefit for our campaign. Coretta Scott King, an ardent supporter of Carter, stopped by The Valley to lend her support and thank me for being a strong advocate for husband Martin Luther King's holiday. My former boss Congressman Charles Rangel visited and lauded my efforts as his intern caseworker assistant. A friend from the old days in Mississippi, Hodding Carter, now spokesperson for the State Department, came by and even contributed money to the campaign. Congressperson Geraldine Ferraro, who was later the first woman to be nominated for vice president on the ticket of a major party made a whistle stop on her way upstate. John Lindsay's daughter returned a favor I'd done for her father by helping to open our campaign office. Lt. Governor Cuomo also dropped by for a quick speech and photo op. Even Mrs. Mondale, the vice-president's wife, visited. Poughkeepsie had rarely seen such excitement.

We actually began to entertain the possibility that we had a chance of winning. When you are surrounded by supporters who are breathing the same rarefied air that you do, such delusions are almost inevitable. When President Carter came to New York City, I was invited to meet him at the airport along with Congressman Rangel, Congresswoman Shirley Chisholm. We greeted him at the airport and traveled to a rally in Brooklyn as part of the Presidential advance team. As a candidate I was invited to the Democratic Party Convention in New York City that summer of 1980.

For the first time in my life, I was inside the convention with credentials. It was filled with all kinds of people: black, white, brown, old, young, men, women, millionaires and welfare recipients, radicals, and conservatives. The Democratic Party was the embodiment of the American experiment. For a short time, we not only "all got along", we were celebrating the fact that we do. The convention pumps blood through the veins of the American dream. To be there is to be inspired to believe that democracy is possible.

I was on the floor for the Ted Kennedy speech. Most agreed that if he had been able to find that fire six months earlier he would have given Carter a real run for the nomination. I was escorted around the New York delegation and introduced to the party leaders. I talked with nationally known Democrats and other celebrities. It was a heady time. I participated in a press conference for obscure upstate candidates. I was even invited to a White House Conference on Agriculture where I had the audacity to propose a coalition of family farm owners and farm workers to promote mutual interests.

Once the convention was over, we were back in the trenches, knocking on doors and holding voter registration drives. Our district covered parts of six counties. I pledged to visit every one of them regularly. Most of the district consisted of small rural towns which, to say the least, were not racially diverse. I remember visiting a volunteer firemen's picnic in a small town in southern Dutchess County. I walked around shaking hands and smiling at babies. I noticed a man toting a Bud following me around, acting strangely. I was getting a little worried, and some of our campaign workers thought I had better get out of there. As I began my exit, the man rushed up to me, grabbed my hand and said, "You got my vote. Any N--— who has the guts to come up in here is alright with me."

In November I received over thirty thousand votes, more than any other African-American candidate, winner or loser, in New York State that year. But, my opponent got over fifty thousand. In the process President Carter lost. He became the first elected President not to win re-election since Taft. He took the Democratic majority in the Senate down with him. We had all fought the good fight but lost. We had demonstrated that it was still possible to run a grassroots campaign on issues based on the peoples' aspirations. But, the Reagan Revolution, rooted in supply-side, trickle-down economics and repressive social measures packaged as reform was now in full swing. It would be twelve years before a Democrat would come back to the White House, the longest period of one party domination of the White House since Roosevelt.

Charles Dumas, Congressman Charles Rangel and Congresswoman Shirley Chisholm

This poem is taken from NIGERIAN JOURNAL which was based upon the observations, readings, discussions and inspirations I recorded as we traveled with Father George Clements, Chuck Rankin, Ralph Gilmer, Tim Hart, Renault Robinson, Lestor Pryor, and Ron Worthy, during a trip to Nigeria in January 2010

MORNING IN IMEKO

Here the day does not begin with drums summoning ancestral spirits, or gun shots vanquishing foes. It does not begin with anguished screams from the parched throats of starving or diseased children, as some would have us believe represents all of Africa. It doesn't.

The African morning here begins with exponentially increasing questions and too few answers. This African morning begins with the clip-clop, clipity - clop of cow hooves on asphalt roads as herdsmen drive their herds to pasture brandishing staffs shorter than the cows' horns.

Followed soon by roosters, sensing the sun rising behind the horizon, they crow from faith which is difficult to find in myself.

Our African almost- morning continues in the darkness.
Shrill calls to prayer are pumped from numerous amplified minarets, each unique but each with common purpose to chant the community into wakefulness. No other church bells ring.

Generators jump start and begin to crank out spots of artificial light in anticipation of the sun. (The early bird catches the worm only if he can see him.)

Down the road, in front of container houses and wooden shacks, stick fires crackle as water is heated for washing, coffee, fu-fu, and preparing fish head pepper soup.

The first cycloped scooters head to the highway, avoiding the soon coming morning traffic jam.

No sun light yet. People trudge along in darkness, some with flashlights, others finding their way, following habits and instincts. Occasional greetings

"Good morning" "How was your night?" God grant you blessings this day"

The stars are still visible. No - more than visible- blazing -

reducing the fires, flashlights, headlights and generators to little more than an afterthought.   The sun- not- yet, but golden angel clouds hint at its imminent arrival, We stretch in the darkness awaiting to do homage and flash proper recognition signals.

Except, for the persistent roosters, no birds sing. No bird's song breaks the Nigerian silence.

Afraid? … Of what? Certainly not the calls to prayer.
 Having gathered at dusk to bid farewell, the birds, too, should be privileged to sing praise songs to summon the seemingly reluctant sun.

Yet they are silent in the presence of clip-clopping cattle and cranking generators.

Perhaps lost ? In a lingering despair born of centuries of misuse, ill use and just plain abuse of the earth and its African people. The darkness which has surrounded them so long, has perhaps seeped into their sinews and strangled their song.
Arise birds and sing. It is a new day coming. Pierce the thickened air with your tintinnabulation, Let your songs fracture the bones of brutal night.

Arise brother birds and sing. Shake the pompous stars, send them into exile or let them quiver in the darkness hidden by our brightening day.

Arise sister birds and sing. Show cousin rooster that his feeble cackle is not the standard by which our orchestral symphonies will play.

Arise birds and sing, sing, sing. Let your song help my heart take wing and I will try to add my meager voice to our grand chorus.

As of this writing there is increased sectarian violence going on in Nigeria. Churches and mosques have been bombed and burned. People have been killed in what appears to be religious based antagonisms.

Timbuktu Diary *Voices, January 2000*

IN THE DESERT OUTSIDE TIMBUKTU, MALI, December 31, 1999
We have come here on camels with our two guides. We pitched our borrowed tent near a bramble bush that offers little shade as the sun moves silently and quickly across the sky. We have only what we could carry, which includes, the tent, blow-up mattress and the two changes of clothes, our food, the cameras, and that most important of necessities–water. The City is not visible any longer on the horizon. All we can see are the barren hills and dunes, a few trees, if you can call them that. We aren't too far from the salt cavern route, which has been the same for a thousand years–traveling from Timbuktu to the salt mines to the north, carrying goods and people and history. It is over a hundred degrees Fahrenheit but not too uncomfortable as long as you keep drinking water. The desert is not empty; it is filled with life, struggling to survive. Earlier today I spent two hours watching three ants take a dropped grain of rice back to their home. There are Tuareg herders about half a kilometer from us. We can see their tent. Pitched low, it hugs the hot ground as if it were resting after a long walk.

We visited them earlier. They served us mint tea while we asked questions about their life: how many sheep, how far do they travel, how long do they stay, where do they go from here? They asked us the same questions. It was more difficult for us to respond than it was for them. A few days ago I asked a man to pick three things that he thought were good in his culture in Mali. He listed (1) His people had a strong belief in God. They pray at least five times a day. God is part of everything that they do, he said. (2) The importance of the family. After God, the family is all; the individual is known and supported by that family. He could not understand how Bill Gates could exist, because he has no family of Gates'. (3) Respect for the elderly. They are the source of our strength, the connection to the ancestors. He asked me the same question.

Yesterday a group of Americans flew in from Los Angeles on a private jet. They were picked up at the airport using nearly all of the four-wheel-drive vehicles in town, whisked down the one paved road to the "deluxe hotel," fed couscous. Then they had turbans wrapped on their heads, climbed up on camels, had their pictures taken. It was off to the museum and a mosque, to the library, and back to the plane and off to Istanbul for the next leg of their round the world millennium trip. They were in Timbuktu for four hours. They spoke to no one but themselves and a few of the merchants to buy souvenirs. Our friends asked us if that is what Americans are like. At first I denied it, but I wonder.

We consume a third of the world's resources while producing very little of basic value except food, which we over-process. We own more of nearly everything than we could ever use. Even in our own lives we come quickly and depart even sooner. We don't take time to take account.

This is not the Africa of the movies, nor is it the Africa of the TV documentaries or charity pitches. I am not surrounded by wild animals or starving children. Rather, I am privileged to witness a culture that is as old as history as stable as a mountain. People find a way to live and survive–no, they thrive. I have held in my hands books printed before there was an English language, before there was an England to have a language. I have drunk water from wells dug by the offspring of the Prophet. I have prayed in Mosques built before Europeans came to capture and shackle our people.

I know why Holy people come to the desert. God is so evident here. Each grain of sand shows the hand of the divine. There is a tree that I sat under for hours, sitting in the middle of a dune. A little fire and it would be a burning bush. This is the kind of land that Moses walked on. This is a hill like Jesus taught from. Elijah heard the wind speak in a place like this. Is that John the Baptist coming over the hill? A thousand years ago this was one of the most important cities in the world. In the 1200s there was a university here which had 25,000 students. The library contained more volumes than any in the world. At a time when our English foreparents were just recovering from the latest Norman invasion, Malian kings were sending caravans all over the known world, and perhaps even the unknown one. Now Mali is one of the five poorest countries in the world based on GNP. The desert is swallowing up the City and its citizens are powerless to stop it. America, my beloved country, heed the lessons of history. Greatness is transitory and fame is fleeting.

EVENING: The temperature has dropped seventy degrees. It is forty outside the tent. There is no sound but our sleeping and the ever-present wind. We will get up and watch the sunrise from our hill, the last one of this century.

Phi Beta Kappa Graduation, Penn State University, May 4, 2012
Thank you for that lovely introduction.

I was wondering why I had been feeling so tired. I have been busy. Of course, if you are closer to being seventy years old than you are to sixty, it means you have had a lot of opportunities to keep busy, to try things, to risk new things. Sometimes you are successful and sometimes you mess up. Fortunately at events like these they only list the circumstances where you have been successful. If they were to list the failures and the mess ups, we would be here all day....

I wasn't Phi Beta Kappa when I graduated from State University of New York back in 1975. You had to be Summa cum laude to be eligible, which at the time required a 3.90. I had a 3.87 cum. No matter how much I groveled I couldn't get the one C I had gotten -in sophomore biology-changed to a B. Anybody that tells you it doesn't matter. Tell them that they are wrong. It is been almost forty years and I still remember why I didn't make it summa. And I remember the teacher who gave me the C. But, you didn't have to grovel, beg, or plead. You got your PBK pins the old fashioned way – as my friend John Houseman used to say – YOU EARNED IT!

Since I am clearly not the smartest guy in the room, I was curious as to why I was asked to come and talk to you on this auspicious day? After all we have Nobel laureates on this campus who could have enlightened you. Barry Marshall could have told you how he discovered the bacteria that caused stomach ulcers, or my friend and colleague Michael Mann could have demonstrated how global warming is real, and we humans are causing it. He would tell you that unless we find alternatives to fossil fuels, the State of Florida might become an underwater coral reef in fifty years. Preparing the speech I thought a lot about this. Why me? I finally came up with an answer. It may not be THE answer but it is in an answer.

I teach in Africa. - Mali, Senegal, Ghana. South Africa. On the continent, people go to great efforts to invite the old people of the village to attend and witness important ceremonies- weddings, births, inaugurations, and graduations. Once the important business is taken care of, the oldest of the old people, an elder, is asked to say a few words to bless and honor the ritual. It is assumed that the elder, the one in the room most proximate to joining the ancestors, has a unique wisdom to add to the ceremony. It is also true that being the oldest means that he or she has the least energy and will not prolong the event too much. The last thing you want is to be forced to sit and listen to some young guy rant on and on about the nature of the universe during your moment in the spotlight. So though I am not the smartest guy in the room I am probably the oldest. So here goes. I have five points of advice.

The first three things I have to say I borrowed from Prof. Jonathan Jansen, the head of the University of the Free State in South Africa. Whenever he is present he is the smartest guy in the room. He is one of the most enlightened educators I have ever met. Prof. Jansen borrowed his advice from a yet older source, the Bible. Professor Jansen at this year's graduation passed on advice he distilled from the Prophet Micah; *He was one of the Minor Prophets from the Older Testament.* His most famous sound bite was chapter 4 verse 3 which reads: *He shall judge between many peoples and shall arbitrate between strong nations far away; they shall beat their swords into plowshares and their spears into pruning hooks; nation shall not lift up sword against nation, and neither shall they study war nay more; but they shall sit under their own vines and under their own fig trees, and no one shall make them afraid, for the mouth of the lord of hosts has spoken."*

But Prof. Jansen chose another verse to share with the South African graduates. First a little background- Micah lived at a time when Israel and Judah were under siege from both external and internal forces. Externally they were under attack by many enemies. In fact the Israelis were defeated and taken into bondage by the Babylonians. Micah admonished the leadership for turning away from the word and teachings of Yahweh and turning toward idolatry and worship of money. He also denounced them for abusing the poor and helpless. Sound familiar?

When those few who had remained faithful asked Micah what

they should do, they probably expected practical solutions- like make lots of money, grow sheep for religious sacrifice, develop the nation's military might so they could defeat the Babylonians, grow more wheat to lower the national debt, develop the infrastructure to create jobs. But, that is not what he said. He didn't articulate national political or economic policy. Instead, He gave them three guidelines by which to live their lives. He said -

1. DO JUSTICE 2. LOVE MERCY 3. WALK HUMBLY WITH YOUR GOD.

Some were confused. It seemed simple. But, upon reflection, they realized it was more complex. And it was difficult to follow. Particularly for those who are used to being the smartest guys and gals in the room.

Do Justice. Justice requires equality. It is the opposite of elitism. And it flows in the opposite direction from competition. To do justice requires you to ask the question, how may I help my neighbor, not how may I defeat him. Do justice. Without justice there is no peace. Those who have been treated unjustly will be in a constant state of turmoil and unrest. Those who treat others unjustly will have their hearts in a constant state of turmoil and unrest. Ask yourselves - Is it **just** that men and women who do the same job get paid different amounts? Is it **just** that immigrants seeking jobs to feed their families are abused and neglected? Is it **just** that we Americans who produce less than ten per cent of the world's goods consume more than a third of its resources? Seek justice and then do justice.

Love Mercy - Beyond the issue of fairness there is mercy. If we all got only what we deserved we would have very little indeed. We couldn't have made it through childhood without the love and mercy of our parents. None of us would have survived the selfishness of the terrible twos, the fearsome fours, and teenage self focused angst unless those who loved us showed us mercy. We have what we have, because at some point someone showed us love. We are who we are because we were shown mercy. The source of mercy is compassion and the knowledge that we all share this planet. No one owns it. We share it as a community. And remember what goes around will come around.

The last is perhaps the toughest one – *Walk humbly with your God.* I don't care if you call your God -Yahweh, Jehovah, Allah, Jesus, or the greatest consciousness of the Universe. Find her and walk humbly with her. The fabricated myth of self-made success, lifting yourself by your bootstraps is a fallacy. None of us got to where we are by just our own efforts. We live on God's made earth, in a human created society. You are graduating from a public land grant University, created by our ancestors' collective effort. Many people had to go through great sacrifices so that you could be here.

How many of you will be the first in your family to graduate from college? You should be especially humble. I am like you. In fact I am the first in my family to actually attend college. I was able to do so because I had the opportunity not because I somehow lifted myself by my bootstraps. I would have had no boots unless parents had brought them so I could survive the cold and deep Chicago snows. They survived because my grandmother cleaned people's houses for a living. She scrubbed toilets so her family would have food on the table. I wouldn't have been able to go Yale Law School in the 70's, if thousands of other people hadn't marched in the 60's to open up the opportunity to all of God's children, black and white. Walk humbly. Walk as if you got here with help. Because you did.

The fourth thing I have to say is something you have heard before. *Follow your joy. Follow your heart.* Back in the sixties there was a popular saying – DO YOUR OWN THING. It was a particularly selfish response to a period of social activism that rocked some of the foundations of society. I don't mean that. Don't tune in, turn on and drop out. Tune in – for sure- tune into the world around you, tune into your own heart. Turn on – sure- but that doesn't mean light up a joint. It means turn on to the immense possibilities that are in the world for you. Don't just look for a job. Try to find a calling. A job will pay your rent; put food on the table, help pay off that student loan. But, a true calling will satisfy that greater hunger in your souls to fit in and contribute to what is right and beautiful in our world. I was an artist.

Then for practical reasons, I went to law school. I was good at the law but it was not my joy. I made money, paid the mortgage, got the kids through college. But, there was something missing. When I got the opportunity to try to pursue my joy in the theatre again, I consulted with my partner and wife. She agreed and we tried it. Thirty years later I can tell you, it was the right thing to do.

The final kernel of wisdom that I will pass on, I take from our campaign slogan. I am running for Congress in this election. Don't worry I am not going to make a campaign speech. Most of you couldn't vote for me any way because you won't be living in this district in the fall. But, I will share with you our slogan. It is – **DON'T QUIT.**

When you graduate things might be a bit rough– but - **Don't quit.**

Don't quit on our University. We had a rough time last year. We have walked a difficult road together. But we have survived and I promise you we will continue to thrive. Never forget you have gone to one of the finest Universities in the world, We are -Penn State.

Don't quit on yourselves- You are our best, you are the future. There is a sacred promise each generation makes – to make sure the world you pass on is better than the world you have inherited.

Don't quit on your dreams. For as Langston Hughes said. "Hold fast to your dreams, for when dreams die, life is a broken winged bird that can not fly"

Don't quit on America. We have the oldest and the greatest Democracy the world has ever known, but, we are still a work in progress. It can get better. You are the sculptors that will mold and shape the new Jerusalem which still inspires hope in the hopeless, still provides visions to the visionary, still empowers the powerless, and still provides a path for those who would walk for justice and mercy.

Don't quit !

In closing I would like share a poem I wrote years ago. It shares the thoughts and feelings of one of those who also had a dream. It is called

Nontraditional Casting:

-The real life emperor of our unreal world barks at me in the dark,
"Don't you know anything about acting Shakespeare?"
My tears dammed by tighten jaws, I escape from that stage, the theatre
to go to the park to sit under a tree to sickly to shade my shame
remembering:
"Don't you <u>know </u>anything-"
And realizing, no, I don't really know anything
Tearing off the tunic, the tears again try to come.
For solace I dig back into childhood – being black, poor, living moment
to moment off fantasies to flimsy to be called dreams. Then as I grew
to Blackmanhood and watched frighten damsels in their distress see
me and run across the street to avoid contact and self created danger. I
Watched old people tighten grips on their near empty purses. I
Watched rookie cops nervously fondle their pieces as I stared them
down packing nothin' but ATTITUDE.
Their fear was like my air-water- source of my substance. Without
that I might have been truly invisible. The only art I had was my
screaming or the gleaming steel walls of subway cars which presented
a canvas for my mark.
UNTIL
This man came to the lower depths of my tenement cemetery and
showed me Hamlet on a bare stage making me realize that I wasn't the
first son who didn't have the balls to avenge his father's murder. He
showed me Macbeth in borrowed costumes so I could see what
happens when ambition isn't kept in check. And I groaned with
Othello, yet another African gone crazy lost in a world not of his
choosing or his making.
Then step by step, line by line, word by word, syllable by metered
syllable, I crawled onto that stage and learned to scream my rage in
iambic pentameter- learned to walk that walk wearing togas and kilts -
learned to stay real, feeling unreal in a totally not real situation.
So, new, refreshed with remembering, I return to answer the question
"Don't you know anything about acting Shakespeare?"

To say, Yes with my tentative Elizabethan tongue.
To shout Yes with my pounding African heart
To proclaim Yes and to fight for a chance to toss my kissed roses,
thorns only slightly, blunted to This waiting world."

Thank you. -- Don't quit. Don't quit,
Don't you ever Quit!

-Charles Dumas, July, 2012

**President Obama Inauguration
January 2009, Washington, D.C.**

References

Dumas, Charles (2009, March) What is a Baobab, Center Daily Times, p.1C.

Dumas, Charles (2009, August) Mending Nets, Center Daily Times, p.1C.

Dumas, Charles (2009, July) FREEDOM: The Fourth of July, Center Daily Times, p.1C.

Dumas, Charles (2009, June) Juneteenth, A Celebration of Freedom, Center Daily Times, p.1C.

Dumas, Charles (2009, February 20) MLK in State College, Center Daily Times, p.1C.

Dumas, Charles (2011, January) Memorials to Dr. King, Center Daily Times, p.1C.

Dumas, Charles (2009, May) Confirm Sotomayor, Now, Center Daily Times, p.1C.

Dumas, Charles (2010, December) Charlie Rangel, Center Daily Times, p.1C.

Dumas, Charles (2011, November) We Are Penn State, Center Daily Times, p.1C.

Dumas, Charles (2010, January) Chaos or Community, May 2010 Center Daily Times, p.1C.

Dumas, Charles (2009, April) The Village, Center Daily Times, p.1C.

Dumas, Charles (2009, July) Not Here, Not Now, Center Daily Times, p.1C.

Dumas, Charles (2010, July) Save Webster's, Save Ourselves, Center Daily Times, p.1C.

Dumas, Charles (2009, October) Open Community, Center Daily Times, p.1C.

Dumas, Charles (2011, December) Give Peace a Chance, Center Daily Times, p.1C.

Dumas, Charles (2009, August) The Spirit of Cahir Should Live On, Center Daily Times, p.1C.

Dumas, Charles (2009, September) Mayor Welch, Center Daily Times, p.1C.

Dumas, Charles (2010, March) Coquese Washington, Center Daily Times, p.1C.

Dumas, Charles (2012, February) JoePa, Center Daily Times, p.1C.

Dumas, Charles (2012, January) A Time for Every Purpose Under Heaven, Center Daily Times, p.1C.

Dumas, Charles (2011, December) THE LARGER COMMUNITY: The Reitz Four, Center Daily Times, p.1C.

Dumas, Charles (2011, July) Oprah in Africa, Center Daily Times, p.1C.

Dumas, Charles (2010, June) Ateqnohkew Pemohneau, Center Daily Times, p.1C.

Dumas, Charles (2010, September) Shalom, Center Daily Times, p.1C.

Dumas, Charles (2011, February) The Social Revolution in Egypt, Center Daily Times, p.1C.

Dumas, Charles (2010, February) Project Haiti, Center Daily Times, p.1C.

Dumas, Charles (2009, May) A Man's Glorious Life, Center Daily Times, p.1C.

Dumas, Charles (2010, March) Good Health Care is A Right, Center Daily Times, p.1C.

Dumas, Charles (2011, August) Death and Taxes in Modern America, Center Daily Times, p.1C.

Dumas, Charles (2011, October) Taking Action Against Cancer, Center Daily Times, p.1C.

Dumas, Charles (2010, November) Leadership Punts New Day Dawns, Center Daily Times, p.1C.

Dumas, Charles (2009, April) THE ARTS: This I believe, NPR, WPSU-FM.

Dumas, Charles (2009, December) The Gods Must Be Crazy-Comments on Celebrity, Center Daily Times, p.1C.

Dumas, Charles (2011, May) Martin Sheen, Center Daily Times, p.1C.

Dumas, Charles (2011, June) Athol Fugard, Center Daily Times, p.1C.

Dumas, Charles (2011, April) Sidney Lumet, Center Daily Times, p.1C.

Dumas, Charles (2009, February) The Wiz, Center Daily Times, p.1C.

Dumas, Charles (2009, March) The Last Poets Reunion, Center Daily Times, p.1C.

Dumas, Charles (2010, October) Unstoppable, Center Daily Times, p. 1C.

Dumas, Charles (2010, June) First Francis Foster Award, Center Daily Times, p.1C.

Dumas, Charles (2009, April) President Obama, My Homie, Center Daily Times, p.1C.

Dumas, Charles (2009, May) My Homie, Part 2, Center Daily Times, p.1C.